MW01173348

Welcome To America

How Cultural Marxism is Slowly Destroying America

From the Co-Authors
of
*37 Days: The Disenfranchisement of a Philadelphia
Poll Worker*

Daryl M. Brooks

Stephen Martino

"We cannot expect the Americans to jump from capitalism to communism, but we can assist their elected leaders in giving Americans small doses of socialism, until they suddenly awake to find they have communism."

— *Late Soviet Premier Nikita Khrushchev*

CONTENTS

ACKNOWLEDGMENTS

Daryl M. Brooks

My mother Janie Brooks and father Robert Griffin. Children Dimonique Brooks, Julion Jacobs, Naji Brown and Iman Sasha Brown Brooks. Grandkids Malik Bell and Little Janie.

Family in Saint Mary's GA. The Wilson's, Myers, Jones and Johnson's.

Special shout- Pastor Greg Locke, Jaunlette Simmons and family, Kathy McBride and family, Barbara Gonzals and family. Nate Jones Jr., Steve Martino, George Hathaway, Joe Siano, Lou Jaskoff, Brig. Gen. Douglas R Satterfield.

My hero's Dr. Martin Luther king Jr., Dr. Bernard Lafayette, Nate Jones Sr., Father Brian McCormick, Rabbi Gordon Geller and Doc Long.

Stephen Martino

With great appreciation, I would like to thank my Dad, John Martino, for the content editing of this book. I would also like to thank my Uncle Charles Martino for his exquisite insight and inspirational quotes that he bestowed upon me and my work. As always, it is a great pleasure collaborating with Daryl M. Brooks on all our projects. Lastly, I would like to thank all the inspiration I receive from my That Man is You men's group, my fellow parishioners, my family, Joe, Hehn, and my fellow Knights.

PROLOGUE

What do the books "And to Think That I Saw It on Mulberry Street," "If I Ran the Zoo," "McElligot's Pool," "On Beyond Zebra!" "Scrambled Eggs Super!" and "The Cat's Quizzer" all have in common?

If you guessed that they were all written by the beloved author Dr. Seuss, you would be only half correct. Known for such classic works as "The Cat in the Hat," "How the Grinch Stole Christmas," and "Green Eggs and Ham," Dr. Seuss has become one of the most well-known and beloved children's authors in the entire world. His memorable stories bring many of us back to a simpler, more innocent time in our lives when politics, bills, and daily life stressors were something relegated to just the grown-ups.

If you also guessed that these books had been canceled by the left, you would have gotten the question totally correct. Yes. The left is now canceling particular children's books written by the beloved American author, Dr. Suess. In 2021, Dr. Seuss Enterprises announced that it would no longer be publishing any of these works because they "portray people in ways that are hurtful and wrong."

The conclusion not to publish these books came after a paper distributed in "Research on Diversity in Youth Literature" concluded that Dr. Suess used racist pictures in his works. Their work stated, "In the fifty Dr. Seuss children's books, 2,240 human characters are identified. Of the 2,240 characters, there are forty-five characters of color representing two percent of the total number of human characters." "Of the forty-five characters of color, forty-three are identified as having characteristics aligning with the definition of Orientalism. Within the Orientalist definition, fourteen people are identified by stereotypical East Asian characteristics and twenty-nine characters are wearing turbans."

This study in "Research on Diversity in Youth Literature," published in 2019, examined 50 books by Dr. Seuss and deemed that 43 out of the 45 characters of color had "characteristics aligning with the definition of Orientalism" or the stereotypical, offensive portrayal of Asians. The two "African characters," the study said, both had "anti-black characteristics." "White supremacy is seen through the centering of whiteness and white characters, who comprise 98% (2,195 characters) of all characters. Notably, every character of color is male."

What's next? Is the "Research on Diversity in Youth Literature" going to come out with an inciteful piece on how Dr. Seuss promoted animal cruelty by portraying poor, defenseless cats who were forced to wear unbearably heavy hats and bow ties that cut off circulation to their lungs? Are they going to conclude next that green eggs and ham are offensive to both vegans and vegetarians?

What was even more absurd was that the cat from "The Cat in the Hat" was described by Katie Ishizuka, a founder of the Conscious Kid Social Justice Library, as a racist caricature used to denigrate black people. In her own words, she stated, "The Cat's physical appearance, including the Cat's oversized top hat, floppy bow tie, white gloves, and frequently open mouth, mirrors actual blackface performers; as does the role he plays as 'entertainer' to the white family—in whose house he doesn't belong."

As a result of the findings by the "Research on Diversity in Youth Literature" and other outlets, the Nation Education Association (NEA) shifted the focus of the yearly "Read Across America" efforts to diversity instead of Dr. Seuss. No longer promoting the works written by the beloved American author, the effort will now be promoting multiculturism and diversity.

Even President Biden fueled the insanity by not mentioning Dr. Seuss in the "Read Across America" presidential proclamation. As a matter of tradition, such former presidents as Donald Trump and Barrack Obama previously paid homage to this great author by mentioning him on this National Day of Reading. "Read Across America Day" was started on March 2, 1998, and has been celebrated on that date since its inception. This date was specifically chosen as it represented Theodor Seuss Geisel's, Dr. Seuss's, birthday.

Another famed American author, Ray Bradbury, could not have penned a better prologue to his classic, "Fahrenheit 451," than the rise and the collapse of Dr. Seuss. In his novel, he portrayed a dystopian society whereby the all-powerful government burned all books to promote ignorance and overall conformity to the state. Such book burning was justified by the government as a response to decreased attention spans and increased protests against a variety of books' contents. In order to prevent future trouble, all books were summarily deemed illegal and burned on sight. To make matters worse, the entire population had been dumbed down by constantly watching television and were unable to think intelligibly for themselves.

Though written in 1953, the tale penned by Ray Bradbury seems all too real today. What once was thought of as absurd has now become a possible reality. As America and the entirety of Western culture continues to implode each day, most continue to ignore the problem. They do nothing, as if they were as mindless and apathetic as the characters portrayed in "Fahrenheit 451."

The mainstream media, American school system, colleges, and universities, TikTok, Facebook, Twitter, and Instagram have all dumbed down America and created a society suffering from short attention spans, poor people skills, an inability to think independently for themselves, and an uncanny susceptibility to being swayed by popular opinion and culture. We are now living in the dystopian future that Ray Bradbury warned us about 70 years ago.

Welcome to America!

CHAPTER 1
INTRODUCTION TO
CULTURAL MARXISM

Many Americans and much of Western civilization have become prey to what I call the Rip Van Winkle Effect. To those who have not heard the story of Rip Van Winkle, it was a short tale by Washington Irving, published in 1819. Set in the American Catskills, it described the infamous account of a humble Dutch farmer who went by the name of Rip Van Winkle. Wanting to escape his overbearing wife, Rip did his best to avoid his duties on the farm and do odd jobs for his neighbors. He would also frequent the local pub, named after King George the Third of Great Britain, to gossip with his friends.

One day, Rip decided to go into the woods with his trusted dog and rifle instead of going to the pub. While hunting, he ran into a bunch of strangely dressed men with long, colorful beards. After imbibing a little too much liquor with them, he fell fast asleep. When he awoke, he found himself incredibly sore and noted that he had grown a long beard during his slumber.

Rip meandered back to town only to note both the entire place and the people had changed. Plus, his old home, once tidy and neat, had become run down. There, he learned that he had slept for 20 years and that his former life had passed. In fact, the pub he frequented had a painting of General Washington under it instead of King George the Third.

What Rip Van Winkle did not realize was that he slept through an entire revolution, the American Revolution, without knowing it. Before falling asleep, King George the Third was ruler over the 13 colonies. Now, President Washington presided over these newly formed 13 states.

Are most of us not like Rip Van Winkle? An entire revolution is occurring right here in America and throughout the entirety of Western civilization, and we are all sleeping right through it. Western culture and its values are being transformed on a daily basis while we blindly watch, almost in slumber, as the fabric of Western civilization is pragmatically destroyed.

It's time to wake up. We are going through a revolution, a cultural revolution, at this very moment, and most of us do not even realize it. If we continue our slumber, we will all soon wake up and find that America and all of the Western civilization have changed dramatically.

You'll all be looking around, wondering what happened. What happened was that the entire revolution took place. The democracy, freedoms, and independence we once enjoyed will be gone. Free thought and speech will be a thing of the past.

Unlike most revolutions that use guns, other weapons, and manual force to create change, the revolution going on in front of us utilizes none of those tactics. Instead, they employ what is known as Cultural Marxism to carry out their goals. The problem is that most people have never heard of the term Cultural Marxism nor fully understand what it means. Those on the left who recognize its tactics are quick to debunk the existence of such a concept and are apt to label it as a far right-wing conspiracy theory. In fact, *Wikipedia* defines Cultural Marxism as "a far-right antisemitic conspiracy theory which claims that Western Marxism is the basis of continuing academic and intellectual efforts to subvert Western Culture." It also goes on to blame alt-right instigators such as former President Trump, Jordan Peterson, and Andrew Breitbart for its dissemination.

Wikipedia also defines the alt-right as a bunch of white supremacists, white nationals, and neo-Nazis. In other words, *Wikipedia* views all people who believe in the horrors of Cultural Marxism or who disagree with the status quo set forth by the mainstream media and purveyed throughout many American college campuses as white supremacists.

Former President Barack Obama summed up very nicely the goal of Cultural Marxism. In his words, he stated in 2008, "We are five days away from fundamentally transforming the United States of America."

Cultural Marxism can be considered a destructive or nihilist theory. Instead of describing what it stands for, the premise behind it is to define what it stands against. Its aim is to destroy everything and every institution that makes Western civilization function. It aims to fundamentally transform the fabric of our entire culture by destroying it and creating a new world in its ashes.

However, by its nature, it never describes what would arise after the fall of Western civilization. Unlike Karl Marx, it does not give the premise that a communist utopia will arise as a result of this collapse. It never guarantees a better tomorrow or the elevation of the entire society. Instead, its sole goal is to bring everyone down to the same level so that all can live uniformity in misery, equally together.

In order to destroy Western society, the Cultural Marxist

theory believes that all institutions that make it operate must be dismantled. The entire fabric of society needs to be undone. In order to do so, its aim is to undermine all of western morality, social structures, religious beliefs, capitalism, patriotism, and the traditional family unit.

Institutions such as the church, law enforcement, the legal system, marriage, and the American government are the first, among many other Western "gold standards," that needs to be abolished.

The Cultural Marxist's goal is to divide people into two groups, the oppressed and the oppressors. Therefore, it labels all Western institutions as intrinsically oppressive. No matter what the institution, they claim that it maintains its authority by oppressing another minority group in order to continue the status quo. Everyone is considered a victim or victimizer in their worldview. Without oppression, Cultural Marxists suggest these institutions would cease to exist as we know them. Therefore, they demand that these institutions, due to their fundamentally oppressive nature, be dismantled.

One example of this strategy is to label all Western institutions as inherently racist. As they were created in a time of slavery or had even the remotest relationship directly or indirectly to the practice, they are all considered innately flawed from the start. Therefore, Cultural Marxists believe they must cease to exist as a result.

Just like in classical Marxism, the ends justify the means to the Cultural Marxist. If the end result is destruction, the means by which it occurs is considered redundant. Therefore, ethical considerations, morality, and even facts are all thrown by the wayside. They would rather watch black inner-city communities burn to the ground to propagate their oppression/victim narrative than do what is right and help these communities solve their problems. It is easier to allow homes, businesses, and people's lives to go up in flames to prove a point, such as all cops are all racists than to lend a helping hand.

As Winston Churchill once said, "Never let a good crisis go to waste." Cultural Marxists take this statement literally. For example, during the George Floyd riots that raged across the country, pallets of bricks mysteriously began showing up around major cities.

In the words of the Kansas City police department in a Tweet to the public, "We have learned of & discovered stashes of bricks and rocks in & around the Plaza and Westport to be used during a riot," KCPD tweeted. "If you see anything like this, you can text 911 and let us know so we can remove them. This keeps everyone safe and allows your voice to continue to be heard."

Kansas City was one among many of our great US cities to have these bricks inexplicably appear during intense racial tension. Did mass protests and political unrest coincidentally make contractors want to start building brick edifices in the middle of the most contentious parts of America? The answer is an overwhelming no. They were put there for a purpose, and that purpose was what the Cultural Marxists wanted the most—destruction.

Reverend Dr. Martin Luther King once stated in a famous speech, "I have a dream that one day on the red hills of Georgia, the sons of former slaves and the sons of former slave owners will be able to sit down together at the table of brotherhood."

Instead of quality of character, Cultural Marxists base each individual on the color of their skin. Race, gender, religion, and sexual orientation are among other characteristics that also define the person. It is these exact qualities, and exclusively these qualities alone, that they use to identify and quantify each and every individual on the planet. Nothing else matters. It is negligible to them the inner quality of a person. The mere fact remains that if they are in a certain ethnic group or have a particular sexual orientation, their beliefs, habits, and oppressive status are predetermined. Nothing else matters about the individual.

The Cultural Marxists' control over their perceived reality must be absolute. Those that speak out against them are demoralized, and all opposing thoughts are considered "hate speech." Dissent is not allowed, and everyone must follow blindly without allowing for original thought.

Therefore, the goal of the Cultural Marxists is to relentlessly control their message. To control their message, they must control all forms of media, educational institutions, and even religious organizations. Plus, they must engrain themselves into the American political system to enforce their will.

Has this exact scenario all but already occurred? Look at the mainstream media in America, Canada, and Great Britain. Gander at public school systems and universities. Just look at what the American political left has become.

But what does, as Obama states, "transforming" all Western institutions produce, especially without proposing an alternative? It produces mass chaos, human suffering, and economic despair. The French revolution of 1789 proved that exact point. After overthrowing the established monarchy led by King Louis and Queen Marie Antoinette, France was marred in years of turmoil.

The truth is that history notoriously repeats itself. As Winston Churchill also said, "Those that fail to learn from history are doomed to repeat it." Is America and the West also heading down the ignominious past, as demonstrated by the French Revolution?

The goal of this book is to detail the history of Cultural Marxism, from its rise to its indoctrination of the West. It will also go on to further explain their beliefs, agenda, and tactics to bring down all of Western civilization. To conclude, the book will explain what you can do to save the West from destroying itself and ultimately defeat Cultural Marxism.

Welcome to America!

CHAPTER 2
KARL MARX AND CLASSICAL MARXISM

The origin of Cultural Marxism begins with Karl Marx. Best known for his 1848 pamphlet, "The Communist Manifesto," and the 1867-1883 four-volume publication, "Das Kapital," Marx was a German philosopher and economist whose ideas and theories still impact us to this day.

Though born to a Christian family, Marx considered himself a devout atheist and ardently disavowed God. In fact, he described religion as "the opiate of the masses." He believed God and religion dulled the senses of the people and naively led them to accept a life of oppression.

Marx saw humanity locked in a perpetual economic struggle brought on by the shortcomings of capitalism. He perceived that all of humanity was divided into two economic classes. The "haves" and the "have nots." He described the working class as the proletariat and the ones who owned the means of production as the bourgeoisie. In "The Communist Manifesto," he proposed that those with the means of production exploited their workers and monetarily reaped from the work of their labor. He described it as economic exploitation whereby the "haves" would eventually grow richer and smaller in number while the "have nots" would grow poorer and more numerous in number.

As a result of this growing economic disparity, he believed the workers, the proletariat, would eventually revolt against their oppressors and usher in a new communist utopia. The new society would be one without class or social distinction. The means of production would not be held in the hands of an exclusive few but owned by the state. Private ownership and private property would then be abolished. He believed that in such a society, wealth would be distributed evenly and equitably. Marx declared, "From each according to his ability, to each according to his needs."

In 1917, Karl Marx's dream of a utopian society finally came to fruition after the Bolshevik Party, led by Vladimir Lenin, deposed Czar Nicholas II and implemented communism for the first time. In theory, Karl Marx believed that such a revolution would usher in other revolutions throughout Europe and eventually into the United States. However, his belief in a worldwide communist utopia failed to materialize.

Instead of the Russian revolution inspiring workers across the globe to revolt against their "oppressors," the global revolution stalled, leaving many to wonder what had happened. Why did the workers not unite? Why were they not inspired by the great communist rebellion?

The answer lies not only with communism itself, but it also falls directly upon the man who created it, Karl Marx.

Marxist theory, by its inherent nature, kills both a person's motivation to work and their innovation to create. The system provides no incentive to do either. Previously, if a person undertook such endeavors, it would mean the possibility of increasing the financial quality of life for them and their family. However, communism destroyed that initiative. Working hard and hardly working yielded the same outcome. It produced an economy that stagnated and a workforce that labored at the lowest common denominator.

Plus, Karl Marx was an ivory-tower philosopher who created his ideas based on theory instead of practical implementation or lessons provided by history. In fact, a prime example of the flawed nature of the Marxist theory occurred in America during the early 1600s at Plymouth Colony, Massachusetts. In true Marxist philosophy, the Puritans communally worked the fields, and the benefits of the land were shared equally amongst the inhabitants of the colony.

Instead of the intended prosperity, it brought great famine to the land, with the specter of starvation looming over each of them on a daily basis. The proceeds of the land were sparse, and many of the colonies grew resultful toward each other as a result. Collective farming proved to be a complete disaster.

As Governor William Bradford wrote in his "History of Plymouth Plantation," "Young men, that were most able and fit for labour, did repine that they should spend their time and strength to work for other men's wives and children without any recompense."

The bottom line was that the Puritans did not want to work harder if there was no reward for their added labor. Plus, watching the bounties of one's hard work being distributed to another who did not put in the same effort only created hostility. The communal utopia that they were attempting to create proved only to be a living nightmare.

It was not until Governor Bradford assigned a parcel of land to each family that they could individually cultivate did the productivity of the Plymouth colony grow. As Bradford wrote, "This had a very good success, for it made all hands very industrious, so as much more corn was planted than otherwise would have been by any means the Governor or any other could use, and saved him a great deal of trouble, and gave far better content. The women now went willingly into the field and took their little ones with them to set corn, which before would allege weakness, and inability; whom to have compelled would have been thought great tyranny and oppression."

To commemorate their success, they held a great feast in 1621. This feast is remembered each year during the fourth Thursday of November in the United States and is called Thanksgiving Day.

In addition to killing a person's incentive to work, Marx failed to realize the difficulty of creating a massive, centralized planning system that would oversee both the means of production and the distribution of its wealth. Such a system, by its mere size and nature, was doomed to failure. No central organization could plan for all the local needs of a particular geographic region, nor could it account for their ever-changing needs for goods and services. Such a system of governance created only corruption, inefficiency, and economic hardship.

Not only were Marxist theories inherently flawed, but so was the man himself. Karl Heinzen, a fellow revolutionary author, described Marx as "intolerably dirty," a "cross between a cat and an ape," with "disheveled coal-black hair and dirty yellow complexion."

Plus, Marx never created any businesses or was able to earn a living wage for himself or his family. He squandered his wife's dowry and was considered lazy by his contemporaries. If it were not for the financial support of his friend and co-contributor to "The Communist Manifesto," Friedrich Engels, the man would have lived in abject poverty.

Marx was also known to associate with Satanists. In fact, many believed him to have been more than just a devout atheist, instead a notorious follower of Satan. As Marx wrote in the poem "Der Spielmann" ("The Fiddler"):

> *That art God neither wants nor wists,*
> *It leaps to the brain from Hell's black mists.*
> *Till heart's bewitched, till senses reel:*
> *With Satan I have struck my deal.*

It is surprising how such a morally corrupt, intellectually naïve, and financially destitute man could have made such an economic and social impact on the world. There is no wonder that the legacy of communism has been one of terror, death, poverty, and the dismal elevation of human suffering.

The legacy of communism in the 20th century speaks for itself. Over 100 million people died directly at the hands of the communists. It produced famines, poverty, the Berlin Wall, gulags, oppression, fear, and economic destruction. Just think of the horrors committed by Joseph Stalin in the Soviet Union, Pol Pot in Cambodia, Mao Zedong in China, and the Vietcong in southern Vietnam. This is the legacy of Karl Marx. Never was it one of prosperity or of a utopian society.

A failed man with failed ideas can only produce failure.

CHAPTER 3
THE RISE OF THE FRANKFORT SCHOOL

Unlike Classical Marxism, Social Marxism was not a byproduct of Karl Marx. However, the foundation of its theory was based on his writings.

The theory behind Cultural Marxism originated in a school located in Frankfurt, Germany. Originally called the Institute for Marxism, the group changed its name to the Institute for Social Research. Founded in 1923 by Felix Weil, the institute was affiliated with Frankfurt University in Germany. Because of its location, the institute eventually began being referred to as the Frankfurt School.

Prior to its inception, many of the founders attended a Marxist study week in 1922 to discuss the weaknesses of Classical Marxism. Because a worldwide workers' revolt did not occur after the Bolshevik Revolution in Russia, many Marxists there were left with a lingering question of what went wrong. What did their idol, Karl Marx, miss?

Their conclusion was that the proletariat would never rise against their economic oppressors in a capitalist society. Because capitalism did create wealth for all, though asymmetrically, the workers or "have nots" would receive just enough to deter them from an outright revolt.

The dream of ending capitalism was still not dead for them, and they understood that newer tactics would be necessary. Their conclusion was that the only true method to destroy capitalism was to destroy Western civilization itself. Every institution, code of morality, and basic family unit needed to be abolished. It would only be at this time, when the masses had nowhere else to turn, they would trust the state for their total support. It would be at this time when the grasp capitalism held over its people would be broken.

In this proposed society, there was no God. The state and its political philosophies were to be a new religion. Plus, they believed that only in the ashes of capitalism could real social change would occur. However, what exactly that change would be was never fully conceptualized.

A Hungarian Bolshevik by the name of György Lukács chaired the weeklong symposium. Known for his disastrous bout as the People's Commissar for Education in Hungary in 1919, he injected his radical left-wing agenda into the symposium. During his short time as the Commissar in Hungary, he promoted a policy that he called "Cultural Terrorism" to destroy Judeo-Christian values and the basic family unit. His policy introduced a new sex education program to public schools that radically contradicted the moral standards of the day. Free sex and the antiquated nature of monogamy were taught to all schoolchildren. This disastrous policy was quickly dismantled after the overthrow of his political party. Though Lukács never became a member of the Frankfurt School, his beliefs shaped its underlying philosophies.

Max Horkheimer assumed directorship of the school in 1930 and ran it until 1958. His philosophies blended the teachings of Karl Marx, Sigmund Freud, and Charles

Darwin together to promote the idea that, under capitalism, everyone was both psychologically and economically oppressed. He also shifted the focus of the school away from classic Marxist economics to that of culture. Instead of an economic revolution proposed by Marx, he proposed a cultural revolution instead.

He also realized that the overall economic success of capitalism would inhibit workers from uniting against the government. Plus, the possibility of social mobility created by capitalism gave workers the hope of improving their own lives through hard work. Despite capitalism's positives, Horkheimer fervently believed the negatives far outweighed its benefits. In fact, he viewed capitalism as the main obstacle stifling true human enlightenment.

Horkheimer recruited Erich Fromm, a social psychologist, to join the school soon after his tenure. Fromm expanded upon Lukács's radical sexual beliefs. His early writings extolled how sexual orientation was a mere social construct created artificially by society. He taught that masculinity and femininity were also social constructs and that there were no differences between the sexes.

Fromm was also a contributor to the hypothesis of Critical Theory, which was popularized by Horkheimer. The basis of this theory, which will be discussed later in the book, was to criticize everything in Western society. Its objective was to break down all of the institutions that held Western civilization together through this relentless criticism.

Herbert Marcuse joined the school in 1932. Soon after, the institute moved to Geneva after the Nazi takeover. It then settled in Columbia University, located in New York until 1949 before returning to Germany. Marcuse was credited for injecting the Frankfurt School's radical agenda into American universities across the country. He believed that the working class were not the ones to usher in communism. Instead, he focused on students and minority groups as the new revolutionaries. He viewed them as impressionable and malleable. As a result, he believed that they would prove to create the perfect revolutionaries.

Herbert Marcuse, just like the rest of the Frankfurt School's members, was a left-wing radical. He referred to Western civilization and democracy as the "most efficient system of domination." He was the one who had been most credited for injecting the political left with its current-day Marxist views. Marcuse went on to teach at Brandeis University in Boston and the University of California, San Diego.

Another notable addition to the school, recruited by Horkheimer, was German Marxist philosopher and psychologist Theodore Adorno. Notably, Adorno eventually held positions at Princeton University and the University of California, Berkley. He brought to the school the idea that the use of Freudian psychoanalysis was a viable method to bring about the Frankfurt School's concept of social change. He also promoted the idea of sensitivity training and labeling opponents of Cultural Marxists with psychological conditions or identifying them as being fascists.

By the 1960s, the impact of the Frankfurt School could be seen throughout all of Western society. As the political left embraced more of its theories, the school's policies slowly trickled into public schools, universities, businesses, academia, and the mainstream media. In fact, much of our current culture can be traced back to the Frankfurt School's members and their ideas. Unfortunately, their impact on the world grows stronger by the day.

The more Cultural Marxists' beliefs and practices take hold, the more tenuous our society has become. As divorce rates rise, crime increases, religions become forgotten, cops and the overall legal system are condemned, and racial tensions explode, we can see the direct fruits of Frankfurt School materialize before our eyes.

CHAPTER 4
CULTURAL MARCH THROUGH THE INSTITUTIONS

In order to destroy capitalism, Cultural Marxists believe that every institution that constitutes the fabric of Western Civilization needs to be dismantled. Because capitalist ideas are integral to these institutions, they are inherently oppressive and should be destroyed. In order to do so, they preach that society has to be turned upside down. The oppressed need to be the oppressors, while the oppressors now need to be oppressed.

This idea of total societal upheaval was introduced to the Frankfurt School through the writings of an Italian socialist by the name of Antonio Gramsci. It was his belief that if you want to change the economics of a society, you must first change its culture. He believed that economics is downstream from culture as opposed to the prevailing classical Marxist belief that culture lies downstream from economics.

Most of what was contributed to the Frankfurt School and its beliefs by Gramsci came through his "Prison Notebooks," which he wrote when jailed by the fascist dictator Benito Mussolini. In these 30 notebooks covering over 3,000 pages of text, Gramsci promoted a peripherally centered society whereby the outsiders were turned insiders, and the insiders were turned outsiders.

He believed Western culture was the main roadblock stopping the glorious communist revolution. His goal was to replace Judeo-Christian values and beliefs with a new region. This religion would not be based upon God or any coherent moral code. This religion would be one created by the people in the form of government. Instead of turning to religion, people would instead turn to the state. God would not bring them their livelihood; the state would.

In addition to attacking traditional Judeo-Christian values, Gramsci believed that the entirety of Western culture needed to be eroded into nothingness. As the entire culture rotted, Gramsci proposed that people would be less self-reliant and more dependent on the state. When this occurred, it would usher in a great communist state and abolish self-governance. His goal to accomplish this task was a process to which he labeled "The Long March" through Western culture.

He sought to capture the youngest and most impressionable in society first. Therefore, the march needed to go through the public school systems and continue into the newspapers, mass media, literature, and theater. People's minds needed to be infiltrated at all times and with as many means as necessary. This long march would be slow but relentless in nature until it overtook every aspect of Western society. It would only be then when the general public was totally brainwashed, could a true revolution begin.

It was as if Gramsci were the modern-day Nostradamus. What was just a hopeful vision of the past has become the unfortunate reality of today.

Just look at American universities. Marxism, socialism, and communism have become the norm, while conservative values are now the counterculture. Many parents worry about sending their kids off to college for fear that they may return as mini-Marxists. Worse yet, instead of their children receiving a proper education, many parents fear that their offspring will become indoctrinated and brainwashed in these pseudo-Marxist think tanks.

Colleges and universities used to be institutions whereby students were taught how to think. However, many liberal ones instead preach the idea of not "how to think" but instead exactly "what to think." Their libraries are filled with books demeaning both the United States and all of Western culture. They demonize our past and criticize those men and women who created it.

Plus, getting into one of these schools is an exercise in Cultural Marxism. Instead of the scholastic aptitude of a candidate qualifying them for admission, many schools now factor in non-scholastic criteria for their admission process. Instead of centering on a candidate's grades, now a person's race, sex, and even socioeconomic status prove just as significant in determining one's eligibility. Plus, qualifying tests such as the SAT and ACT, which can help aid a school in the admitting process, are considered by the left as racist. The National Association of Education, the same organization that turned its back on Dr. Seuss, wrote, "Since their inception a century ago, standardized tests have been instruments of racism and a biased system." Thus, many colleges and universities have made them optional.

A 2006 survey of American professors showed that 18% of social scientists self-identified as Marxists. It also noted that 24% of these social scientists considered themselves radical. Just think of what the numbers would be today. And these are the professors teaching our children.

A *New York Times* article in 1989 wrote, "As Karl Marx's

ideological heirs in Communist nations struggle to transform his political legacy, his intellectual heirs on American campuses have virtually completed their own transformation from brash, beleaguered outsiders to assimilated academic insiders."

Victims of Communism, a DC-based non-profit, came out with a poll that showed that "70% of Millennials say they are likely to vote for a socialist while one in three view communism favorably." These numbers were substantiated by a study by YouGov that showed that 36% of millennials approved of communism.

A Gallup poll in 2018 showed that 47% of Democrats viewed capitalism positively, down from 56% in 2016. It also showed that 57% of them now viewed socialism positively.

These numbers clearly show how Marxist ideas are infiltrating society and taking hold in people's minds. As Critical Race Theory takes hold in schools, radical sex education has become the norm, and as Marxist ideas infiltrate teachers' unions, our children are getting indoctrinated at even younger ages. It's no wonder why people today are forgetting about the horrors of socialism and communism and naively turning away from capitalism.

The mainstream media has also been infiltrated by Marxism and the Frankfurt School of thought. You can not turn on the television or pick up any publication without becoming inundated with left-leaning messages. Numbers substantiate these claims. Media Tenor, an independent media research firm, showed that only 3% of the stories reported on NBC and CBS about former President Trump were positive. A study by the Media Research Center found that 89% of all ABC, CBS, and NBC evening news coverage were negative to the former president in just his first 100 days.

The print media fared no better in their coverage. Newsweek, Time, and Esquire, to name a few, were relentless on former President Trump. Just compare their depiction of him to his predecessor, Barrack Obama. George Mason and Chapman universities reported that 59% of his press coverage was positive during his first 100 days in office.

No wonder the media is vilified as spewing "False News." Statistics back up these claims. Either through reporting only the negatives or outright lying, such as in the case of the "Hands Ups – Don't Shoot" story, the mainstream media's goal is clearly not to relay the truth. Instead, their agenda has become one originating from Cultural Marxist ideology, with its foundations entirely stemming from the teachings of the Frankfurt School.

Hollywood is but another casualty of Cultural Marxism. Once putting out pro-Christian and Pro-American films to worldwide audiences, Tinseltown has become a mouthpiece for the Cultural Marxists. For example, the Academy of Motion Pictures Arts & Sciences now utilizes what is called the Representation and Inclusion Standards Entry platform (RAISE) to qualify a film for a Best Picture nomination. In order to register for this award, movies now need to register all demographics and personal information of everyone involved in making the film. Plus, the picture must also meet two of their diversity standards.

CBS has created its own racial qualifications to work for its company. They now require that its writers be 50% black, indigenous, and people of color (or BIPOC) for the 2022-2023 season. Qualification is not based on talent or skill as the main criterion. Instead, a strict race-based quota is enforced.

Black, Indigenous, or Person of Color (BIPOC) has become the main qualification standard for employment in

Hollywood. To help enforce the guidelines, filmmaker Ava DuVernay, along with Oprah Winfrey and Taylor Swift, created what is known as the ARRAY Crew. This listing is a database of women, people of color, and others from underrepresented groups now promoted by Hollywood for all their hiring. Many in the industry, such as Jordan Peele, embrace these new standards. He went as far as to say, "I don't see myself casting a white dude as the lead in my movie. Not that I don't like white dudes. But I've seen that movie before."

The Cultural Marxists have set the new standard in Hollywood, and if you don't obey their strict ideology, you are out. It is the reason why many screenwriters, producers, and actors dare not criticize their policies. If they did, they would quickly find themselves out of a job. Just look at what happened to Roseann Barr from her own show and Gina Carano from the *Mandalorian. The Oprah Daily* went one step further by publishing a hit piece in 2020, naming 27 prominent celebrities who supported the Republican party.

Many streaming services are just as passionate about promoting Cultural Marxist beliefs, with Disney Plus standing out on top. With releases such as *Ms. Marvel* and *She-Hulk* blatantly expressing their views, Disney Plus rather push a Cultural Marxist agenda than churn out quality shows. Netflix, on the other hand, took great scrutiny for carrying Dave Chappelle's *The Closer* because of the comedian's anti-trans beliefs.

The figurative march through the institutions has now, regrettably, engrained itself within our government and, worse yet, in our armed services. Instead of being taught how to win wars, some soldiers are indoctrinated into Cultural Marxism ideology. No longer are military recruits taught of America's greatness. As a substitute, they are brainwashed into thinking that our great Founding Fathers' goal in creating the US Constitution was to solidify white supremacy. While other countries' militaries are being drilled on military tactics, our recruits are being taught Critical Race Theory under the guise of equality. As one Air Force spokesperson openly admitted, "Diversity, inclusion and equal opportunity education and training are essential to cultivate positive values and behaviors, as well as an environment where inclusion and equity for all personnel is achieved."

The US armed force's image is used to portray that of a strong American soldier, able to conquer any challenge which stands before them. The Army's ads once boasted, "In the Army, we do more before 9AM than most people do all day." Now commercials on television promote racial diversity and "gay pride." In an animated ad labeled "The Calling," the Army hoped that wokism and diversity would somehow inspire the strongest and bravest to become a proud members of the US Army. No wonder why military recruitment continues to plummet. It has not been this poor since the Vietnam war.

Though General Mark Milley, chairman of the Joint Chiefs of Staff, denies the accusations that the US military has gone "woke," his actions fail to substantiate these fraudulent claims. Instead of wanting to maintain a hard-fought stronghold in the Middle East, he admitted, "I want to understand white rage. and I'm white." How is this mindset going to win a war or help protect American citizens at home and abroad?

It doesn't. Just look at Milley's disastrous loss and retreat from Afghanistan. All that the Americans and their allies fought for and all those lives forever changed or lost as a result of the war was for naught. The entire country imploded under Milley's oversight and abject neglect. It is appalling to think about all the Americans and allies that were stranded during the chaotic withdrawal, left to the brutal whim of the Taliban. Plus, the US Department of Defense estimated that $7.12 billion worth of military equipment purchased by the United States was left in the country, abandoned for the Taliban's taking.

Under Milley's purview, Lieutenant Colonel Matthew was let go from his post as commander of the 11th Space Warning Squadron after writing about how Marxism, under the pretext of Critical Race Theory and diversity training, is infiltrating the US armed forces. Lohmeier also went on to describe his working environment as "hyper-politicized," whereby conservative-minded thinkers were labeled as extremists and potential enemies of the state.

These claims have been substantiated as the Pentagon has begun to monitor the social media accounts of the enlisted to ensure they conform to their "woke" agenda. Their tactics are reminiscent of that of Communist China or of the Marxist Russians, and their goal is to purge conservatives out of the military.

Unfortunately, the march through the institutions has been a complete success for the Cultural Marxists. There is not even one aspect of our lives not touched by their anti-Western sentiments. From the news we see on TV or in print to the military who are trained to protect our country, no institution has been spared the sting of the Cultural Marxists. Even the stores we shop at, including Target and Walmart, and the consumer products we buy, such as from Procter & Gamble and Kellogg's, have been infiltrated. It seems as if the march has gone unabated, and its footsteps are growing louder and with more numbers each day.

CHAPTER 5
CRITICAL RACE THEORY

Many in the media and even the general public question why Critical Race Theory (CRT) is such a hot-button topic. In order to fully understand the danger behind CRT, you must first recognize where it originated and its intended purpose.

CRT stems from an intellectual practice known as Critical Theory, which is the brainchild of the Frankfurt School. First published by the school in a 1937 essay "Traditional and Critical Theory" by Max Horkheimer, it was described as an exercise "to liberate human beings from circumstances which enslave them." And the circumstances to which he warns about is capitalism.

Critical Theory's goal, as outlined by Horkheimer and supported by the rest of the Frankfort School, is to destructively criticize all Western institutions, ideas, and beliefs in an attempt to destroy them. Only through their eradication would the enslavement perpetrated by capitalism on its people come to an end. The objective of Critical Theory is not one of productivity; it is solely an exercise in destruction. The aim of Critical theory is to directly attack Western culture, capitalism, and Judeo-Christian beliefs in order to create change.

However, this practice of intensive social critique does not provide a method whereby the process is at all constructive, informative, or helpful in making any type of positive change. The process offers no process by which constructive modifications can occur, nor does it have a method to critically analyze a situation from different points of view. By its mere nature, Critical Theory is purely a negative exercise meant to destroy what it is against and not to establish what it is for. It seeks to dismantle the fabric of Western society and all institutions, morals, and beliefs that create the inner, vital fabric that holds society together.

The criteria to employ Critical Theory is actually a very simplistic exercise. Its basic hypothesis is that all Western institutions are inherently prejudiced against minority groups. There is no exception to the rule. It is an absolute and dogmatic belief, without exceptions being allowed. Every Western institution is considered an oppressing force, subjugating a minority or "underprivileged group." In an equivalent Marxist analogy, the bourgeoisie is now the "institution," and the proletariat is the "group that is being oppressed." It is basically the same idea as Classical Marxism but modernized for contemporary society.

The practice of applying Critical Theory begins with identifying a particular group or "institution" as the oppressor or as privileged. Anyone else is then designated as the oppressed or in an underprivileged group. In this scenario, those in the oppressor category must accept their assignment without question. They must understand that by their mere existence, they are inherently oppressing a minority group or groups of people. If they deny this designation, the person is said to have internalized their pathology and is negatively labeled by the Critical Theorists. They are then called terms such as racist, homophobe, sexist, misogynist, or xenophobe, for example.

The next step in this practice, as author Alasdair Elder in his book "The Red Trojan Horse" explains, is to create a victim narrative. The goal is to prove how minority groups have been victimized by the majority and how this problem is "systemic." For example, how many times have we been told that the entire legal system and all cops are "systemically racist"?

Using Critical Theory, Cultural Marxists then expand this idea of systemic racism to every institution in traditional Western society. Nothing and no one is spared from these attacks.

To prove how systemic the problem is, Critical Theorists apply anecdotal stories to bolster their argument. The George Floyd case is a prime example. Instead of media outlets addressing a very unfortunate situation appropriately, they blamed the death of George Floyd on the entire institution of law enforcement across the country. They then went on to report on other isolated and anecdotal events to show just how systemic the problem had become.

In retrospect, it is ironic how powerful and influential a force the media has turned into and how adept they are at quickly swaying public opinion. A month prior to the death of George Floyd, the news portrayed cops and other first responders as heroes during the COVID-19 pandemic. As a result, cakes and other gestures of appreciation were sent to the police departments. With a quick change in the media's reporting, instead of cookies being brought to the police stations, Molotov cocktails and bricks were replacing them.

Critical Theory also puts forth the belief that any action perpetrated by a minority group is considered justified because of their wrongful oppression. This example again played out perfectly during the Floyd riots. Instead of condemning the protestors for destroying public property, they were instead portrayed as the heroes in the situation. The news media overall gave them a free pass while their cities and livelihood burned to the ground.

NPR published, "As Officials Condemn Violence During Protests, This Professor Says Some Is Warranted." The Nation came out with "In Defense of Destroying Property." *Teen Vogue* had the audacity to push, "Don't Let Them Bad-Mouth Rebellion or Riots: How We Name Movements Matters." *The Guardian* went on to say, "The George Floyd protests are a rebellion against an unjust system." Instead of condemning such actions, the Critical Theorist not only sympathizes but they justify abhorrent behavior if it is committed by a minority or so-called "oppressed" group.

Finally, Elder points out that for the Critical Theory to be complete, a comprehensive feedback loop needs to be created. This loop is generated by reinforcing the narrative as many times as possible and by as many outlets as possible. Let the public be inundated wherever they go: the internet, newspapers, TV, schools, movies, and radio. Let the message become ingrained in them, whereby it eventually becomes their truth.

Critical Race Theory (CRT) is a prime example of how Critical Theory can be applied. CRT asserts that all Western institutions are inherently racist and that it is a staple of their existence. Originally taught in graduate-level schools, the idea has infiltrated colleges and universities and is now moving into the public school system.

The goal of CRT is to examine everything through the lens of racism. By its nature, it believes racism is ingrained in all institutions. CRT suggests that history can be defined as a power struggle between racist oppressors and disenfranchised minorities. Individuality is not prioritized in such a process. Instead, entire groups of people and their relationships within this racial struggle are examined.

Many refer to CRT as a verb instead of a noun. It is understood why this conclusion can be made. CRT is applied by a relentless negative critique to destroy America, Western history, and the basic institutions that hold them all together. CRT, by its mere nature, does not allow for a growing or learning process. There is nothing in its use that promotes a positive outcome. In the end, all Western institutions and history are portrayed negatively, without exception. One never feels positive about anything that CRT is used to critique.

Director of Racial Studies and associate professor of English and Humanities at the University of Houston-Downtown, Jay Robertson, says, "The goal of CRT is to equip students with the ability to change the systems, structures, and institutions that maintain racial inequities."

He defines CRT into five categories in his "comprehensive curricular approach to K-12":

1. *Race is not biological; it is a sociological construct.*
2. *Racism is a normal, common, and systemic mechanism that racial differences and racial inequalities are maintained.*
3. *Race and racism are "materially deterministic," that is to say, race and racism advantage the dominant group and therefore any racial advancement or racial equity measure will only occur if it benefits the dominant group (in the case of the U.S., white Americans).*
4. *Racial identity is a dynamic process that changes depending on the needs or interests of the dominant group. Different racial groups are racialized differently at different moments in time for different reasons.*
5. *Because of these dynamics, racialized and marginalized peoples have unique insight into the nature of oppressive systems,*

structures and institutions.

This line of thought outlined by Jay Robertson clearly fails to show how CRT will create a positive outcome, nor does it include such a process to do so. Kimberly Fletcher wrote in *Moms for America*, "Critical Race Theory teaches our children to hate their country, neighbors, and themselves."

CRT is the reason why people are toppling down statues of Christopher Columbus and our Founding Fathers while desecrating other monuments our country once revered. Children are being taught to hate their race, color, religion, and sex. They are also being taught that the "American dream" is a fraud. CRT crushes their self-esteem and dreams of a positive future. No wonder why teenage suicide rates are on the rise.

In the journal *JAMA Pediatrics*, it showed that there was five times the increase in suicidal overdoses among children in the 10- to 12-year-old age range over the period of 2000 to 2020. The CDC reported that the suicide rate among kids aged 10 to 24 increased by nearly 60% between 2007 and 2018. Other factors do contribute to these results. However, in the end, these numbers continue to rise.

Another bias of CRT is that birthright alone determines one's future and that whiteness guarantees success, and that being born black dooms one for failure. It grossly fails to rejoice in the accomplishments of black or other minority communities. In fact, it tends to denigrate those of color who succeed in life. These people are called "Passing as White."

Derrick Bell, the father of Critical Law Theory, states, "'Passing' is well known among black people in the United States and is a feature of race subordination in all societies structured on white supremacy. Notwithstanding the purported benefits of black heritage in an era of affirmative action, passing is not an obsolete phenomenon that has slipped into history."

CRT author and professor Ibram X. Kendi goes as far as to state, "The only remedy to racist discrimination is antiracist discrimination. The only remedy to past discrimination is present discrimination. The only remedy to present discrimination is future discrimination." Ironically, this quote can be found in his book, "How to Be an Antiracist."

Another prime example of Ibram X. Kendi's CRT beliefs can be found in his children's book "Stamped for Kids." The objective of this popular book is to teach kids about white supremacy and that slavery was just a European construct. It goes on to explain how former president Lincoln was a racist and how something as concrete as math and science is inherently racist. His example is just one of many of the other "uplifting" CRT children's books on the market.

The sad truth is that these are the books and philosophies being pushed on our youth. What will America and the rest of Western society become if they are taught to hate themselves? The Cultural Marxists had the answer. The West will cease to exist. And that is their ultimate goal.

CHAPTER 6
IDENTITY POLITICS

Wikipedia defines identity politics as "a political approach wherein people of a particular race, nationality, religion, gender, sexual orientation, social background, or other identifying factors develop political agendas that are based upon these identities." Thus, the mere nature of your existence inherently defines every aspect of your life, attitudes, prejudices, and eventual success or failure in life. It completely disregards a person's individuality, thoughts, and actions, while clumping every person into a greater, collective group as a whole.

The Cultural Marxists have slowly shifted political differences from an economic viewpoint to one of social identity. This perspective reiterates their belief that economics lies downstream from culture. Instead of news organizations or politicians concentrating on economic issues and political policies, the thrust of many conversations has now turned to a person's identity.

The end result of identity politics is that it creates an illusion whereby all people are at all times oppressing or being oppressed by another group. It wants to generate this atmosphere of constant tension between the "haves" and "have-nots."

Taken one step further, it generates a victim-minded

mentality, whereby a person creates a mental tally of how victimized they are in Western society. The categories which the Cultural Marxists claim to make a person a victimizer include being white, male, middle- or upper-class, Christian, cis-gender, and able-bodied. The more a person identifies with any of these categories, the more privilege they are considered to possess. The further away a person gets from this privileged status, the more they are considered victimized by society.

For example, the darker a person is, the more their racial identity makes them inherently victimized by society. Thus, blacks would score more points than, say, Arabs in such a category, and an atheist would garner a higher score than an agnostic. The higher your score, the more victimized or marginalized you are by society, and more importantly, the more society needs to pay you retribution for such oppression.

Through "dog whistles," which are intentional aggressions, and "microaggressions," which are unintentional aggressions, a dominant group asserts its authority over an entire marginalized portion of society. An example of a "dog whistle" would be using terms such as "family values," "welfare reform," or "law and order." These terms are believed to deliberately demean a minority group. Microaggressions such as, "I'm not a racist. I have several black friends," asking a non-white person, "Where were you born," or making a statement like, "America is a melting pot," are all also considered a form of domination, though unintended.

As a result, terms like "white privilege" and insults such as "check your privilege" have now emerged in society. These phrases are not meant as a valued critique. Instead, they are designed to shut down opposition and dissenting non-Marxist points of view. Cultural Marxists promote such radical beliefs. In fact, Herbert Marcuse went as far as to say that the majority no longer had any rights, while Theodore Adorno believed that only white Christians could be prejudiced or racist.

It seems as if identity politics has infiltrated everywhere throughout Western society. It is shoved in our faces by the media, politicians, and educational systems. We cannot enjoy even the simplest products without being reminded of Cultural Marxist ideas.

Even an all-American company like Coca-Cola echoed the virtues of the Frankfurt School when they started telling their employees to be "less white." They took this travesty one step further to explain what being "less white" actually entailed:

- be less oppressive
- be less arrogant
- be less certain
- be less defensive
- be less ignorant
- be more humble
- listen
- believe
- break with apathy
- break with white solidarity

No longer is being white just meant to describe the color of your skin. Per Cultural Marxists, it marks your destiny, attitudes, beliefs, and prejudices. Coca-Cola was not the only company to push racist, anti-white sentiments. AT&T Corporation has created a reeducation program whereby employees are taught the statement, "White people, you are the problem." They also go on to teach, "American racism is a uniquely white trait." Disney promotes its own "diversity and inclusion program," which is based upon the belief that the company was built on racist ideas. Therefore, they ask their employees to fill out a "white privilege" checklist.

Even the beloved Home Depot has succumbed to the Frankfurt School's teachings. In Canada, they were handing out an educational pamphlet to their employees about "white privilege." Though the company quickly disavowed this material, their intentions were made painfully obvious.

Certain movements, such as the feminist movement, have turned away from their original objectives and embraced the Cultural Marxist mantra. Originally it was designed, as defined by *Wikipedia*, to be a "collection of movements and ideologies aimed at defining, establishing, and defending a state of equal political, economic, cultural, and social rights for women." By this definition, feminism, at its surface, is a noble movement fighting for equality and justice between the sexes. Plus, as history reminds us, it has generated great and meaningful changes in the fabric of America. In 1920, the US Congress ratified into law the 19th Amendment, which gave women the right to vote. In 1963, Congress passed the Equal Pay Act. In 1972, Title IX of the Education Act was signed into law by Richard Nixon. It stated, "No person in the United States shall, on the basis of sex, be excluded from participation in, be denied the benefits of, or be subjected to discrimination under any education program or activity receiving Federal financial assistance."

Unfortunately, the honorable intentions and noticeable past successes of the feminist movement have been hijacked by the Cultural Marxists. Instead of promoting equality of the sexes, the movement has turned into a militant, anti-patriarchal organization. It denigrates marriage while promoting single, unwed mothers, despite its proven risks of increased child poverty, school delinquency, and scholastic failure. Like the members of the Frankfurt School, feminists of today support the idea that gender is a social construct and believe there are no differences between different sexes. It admonishes inherent male and female traits and belittles women who do not give up their families to join the workforce.

Its hypocrisy, among other examples, became blatantly obvious during the former President Bill Clinton and Monica Lewinsky scandal. Though the feminists were there during the #MeToo movement, they completely ignored Lewinsky during the Clinton hearings. Because the president and his wife were ardent supporters of the Frankfurt School's ideas, they chose to look the other way at a time when Lewinski needed their help the most. Also, where have they been when trans-athletes such as Lia Thomas completely dominated women's swimming events? Thomas won numerous competitions, taking the awards away from the best female-born athletic competitors participating in them. Though Thomas is at an obvious genetic advantage, the feminists again look the other way.

The Cultural Marxists use identity politics to segregate, denigrate, and demoralize. As mentioned earlier, it is meant to turn society upside down. How else better to do it than to undermine the so-called "people at the top" who theoretically maintain society's status quo?

Jane Elliot, a third-grade teacher in Riceville, Iowa, proved in 1968 just how easy it was to psychologically marginalize a group of people. Just as Antonio Gramsci's and the Frankfurt School's goal was to topple the perceived powers of authority and create a peripherally-centered society, Elliot cleverly devised a social experiment to show just how simple manipulating social perceptions could be. Though her motives were different, the outcomes were the same.

In Cultural Marxist terms, Elliot first created an "oppressor group." These were the students with brown eyes. She then created a victimized or marginalized group, all of which had blue eyes. The brown-eyed children were told they were better and smarter and given special privileges. She also went on to chastise the blue-eyed children that they were lazy and that the melanin in the brown-eyed children's eyes made them smarter. These stereotypes were reiterated throughout the day as the teacher enforced her brown-eyed superiority message to the students. As a result, the blue-eyed student's self-esteem, self-worth, and even self-confidence plummeted. They scored worse on tests and overall performance declined.

Though one may write off the experiment as merely manipulating gullible third graders, the test was repeated with similar success in adults. Plus, this experiment has been proven positive when perpetuated on an entire country. For example, take Nazi Germany, when attitudes toward the people of Jewish faith turned sour, and an entire anti-Semitic culture and country arose out of perpetual Nazi anti-Jewish propaganda.

Are the Cultural Marxists not doing the same thing now, not only in the United States but also throughout the entire Western civilization? Are not they forcefully trying to marginalize and debase those that are in a perceived position of power to topple the entire societal structure? Have they not created an atmosphere of alleged oppression at all times?

To promote this stereotype, the Cultural Marxists promote the idea of "safe spaces" to protect the "marginalized and victimized" members of society from the perceived oppression that surrounds them at all times.

The *Oxford Dictionary* defines a "safe space" as a "place or environment in which a person or category of people can feel confident that they will not be exposed to discrimination, criticism, harassment or any other emotional or physical harm." Though originally created with good intent, the Cultural Marxists have perverted the idea of "safe spaces" in such places as college campuses to create an area where free speech and flow of ideas cease to exist while groupthink and victim mentalities flourish.

However, the truth is that these college-based "safe spaces" can do more harm than good. Liz Swan, Ph.D., wrote in Psychology Today, "Safe spaces let us hide in our comfortable little existence, which is dangerous because they prevent us from growing and changing when faced with adversity—creating new neural networks and adapting. And the ability to do just those things is what has kept us alive as a species. The fittest in the competition for survival are those that can adapt in order to face challenges and overcome them."

One of the ultimate goals of the Cultural Marxists and Frankfurt School is to create a society of victims. It's a society whereby no one needs to take responsibility for their actions, and there is always another person or group to blame for their misfortunes. People in this new society look to the outside in search of what is wrong with them instead of turning to themselves. Happiness is believed to be an external event and not internal in nature. It ultimately creates an atmosphere of resentment. It teaches people to believe that the only way a situation could get better is if other people change or if society changes as a whole.

Just like when the colony at Plymouth almost starved to death, the Puritans were expecting others to change their environment instead of taking the initiative upon themselves. This scenario is exactly the right formula for societal collapse. The Cultural Marxists understand this principle and utilize it at its utmost efficiency to destroy Western culture from the inside.

CHAPTER 7
WHAT IS TRUTH

"If your faith in the authority and truth of the Bible change with culture, you never believed it in the first place."
— Pastor Greg Locke

Many of us ask ourselves, "What exactly is the truth?" As news outlets progressively report more of their own opinions and agendas rather than facts, our faith in the media dwindles by the day. When we hear or read a breaking news report, many question its validity and ask as it if it's just another "fake news" story. This cynicism comes from both ends of the political spectrum.

News stories such as the one that came out of Kenosha, Wisconsin, in the wake of the police shooting of Jacob Blake fuels this mistrust. While CNN correspondent Omar Jimenez was reporting in front of a raging fire with destroyed vehicles in the middle of it, CNN ran the headline, "FIERY BUT MOSTLY PEACEFUL PROTESTS AFTER POLICE SHOOTING." This exact type of reporting was parroted in a riot in Minneapolis when Ali Velshi, an MSNBC reporter, said, "I want to be clear on how I characterize this. This is mostly a protest. It is not generally speaking unruly," in front of a burning building.

Our eyes obviously do not deceive us. Both examples are obvious attempts to manipulate the truth in order to create a pre-determined result or agenda. The message the news organizations wanted to portray was that all police are "bad" and racism is inherent throughout all precincts in America. These stories were meant to fuel the anti-establishment, anti-law, and antipolice narrative. With slogans like "defund the police," the Cultural Marxist goal was obvious: to destroy the Western institution known as law and order.

As examples like the ones above inundate us by the day, one must ask, what exactly do the Cultural Marxists consider to be their truths? Max Horkheimer of the Frankfurt School wrote, "Logic is not independent of content." He articulated this point by promoting the idea that all arguments are logical, independent of their content or facts if it destroys Western culture, and illogical if it supports it. Under this mindset, Cultural Marxists adhere to the belief that $2+2=5$ if 5 is the desired outcome. Facts are irrelevant. Truth is based upon desired outcomes, and outcomes are not the logical result of actual truths and facts.

This type of logic supported by the Cultural Marxists explains the mindsets, beliefs, and understanding of those that adhere to its teachings. No wonder why it is so difficult to have a meaningful conversation or exchange of ideas with a Cultural Marxist. Attempting to combat illogic with facts and statistics can prove to be a meaningless endeavor, especially when they respond only with group-think platitudes or biased opinions. Kurt Schlichter in *Townhall* wrote, "There is no best way to argue with a liberal. They're beyond argument. You might as well argue with your terrier. Take it from someone who argues with his hideous terrier all the time."

The goal of the Cultural Marxists is not to have an actual debate. Instead, their objective is to make those who disagree with them surrender to their will. They want to wear them down instead of using facts and statistics to change their minds.

Another prime example of how Cultural Marxists want to promote their truth that all police are inherently racist and need to be defunded was the "Hands Up – Don't Shoot" incident of 2014. It occurred after a white police officer reportedly shot an innocent, unarmed black man, Michael Brown, in Fergusson, Missouri. As described ad nauseum by the mainstream news outlets, Brown had his hands clearly up in the air, surrendering to the police officer, while pleading, "Don't shoot," before he was maliciously gunned down by a racist cop who belonged to a racist police department.

Protests were triggered across the country as a result of the story. It augmented an underlying social unrest that was already brewing in the country. Shirts were made reading, "Hand up, don't shoot," and hashtags on the issue rocketed throughout Twitter. Celebrities like LeBron James joined the fray by helping to publicize the incident while the St. Louis Rams came onto the field holding their hands up in the air.

The irony was that the story was not true. A St. Louis grand jury and a Department of Justice investigation confirmed this conclusion. Over 40 witnesses were questioned, and all the evidence was thoroughly reviewed. The "hands up" narrative proved nothing more than hearsay. The facts bore out that Brown reached for the police offer's firearm and was shot in an act of self-defense after he charged the cop.

Many still use the hands-up gesture to this day. And

despite the initial mass media and social outcry, the truth of what actually occurred in Fergusson was simply mentioned as an afterthought when it no longer met the Cultural Marxists' narrative. However, the damage was done. It was a proverbial black eye on all of law enforcement, which still has not been eradicated. Facts did not matter in this incident. As Max Horkheimer preached, truth "is whatever fosters social change." If the change is the abolishment of the police, the truth is that the cop shot an unarmed, innocent man.

The Cultural Marxists and Frankfurt School take their warped logic one step further. They believe that they alone have a monopoly on truth and that dissenters lack any moral rights to their point of view. In a 1965 essay, "Repressive Tolerance," Herbert Marcuse wrote that there should be tolerance only to the left while complete intolerance to those on the right. The right's views are considered invalid and not worthy of intellectual discussion. He believed the abolition of free speech was necessary and that minority groups required special privileges to protect against oppression. Through the teachings of the Frankfurt School, the new "left" has every right to "the withdrawal of toleration of speech and assembly" from their opponents. All alternative points of view in contrast to those of the Cultural Marxist need to be suppressed.

Marcuse's teaching should come as no surprise, as all across the United States and in many Western countries, free speech and assembly by the "right" are actively being suppressed by the "leftist" Marxists. The University of Scranton denied a chapter of the conservative group Turning Point USA to register on their campus. Milo Yiannopoulos was shouted down by protestors at the UC Berkley campus and was eventually unable to participate in their ironically-labeled "Free Speech Week." Gonzaga University canceled Ben Shapiro's planned talk twice due to intense opposition. These examples are just a proverbial drop in the bucket as to what is going on across college campuses and all Western societies.

Not only do the Cultural Marxists want to censor free speech, but now they also want to intrinsically change speech itself. This effort, thought to have originated from a term mentioned in Mao Tse Tung's "Little Red Book," has come to be known as Political Correctness (PC). The goal of PC is simply to use language as a means of control over people's thoughts, beliefs, and attitudes. Inherently, the Cultural Marxists utilize it to enforce their will upon the masses. Though altruistically advertised as a linguistic method to be more sensitive to all members of society, no matter what race, gender, or sexuality they may have, it is basically a technique to repress free speech and dissenting ideas.

If someone is taught how to speak, teaching them how to think and what to believe is that much easier. The great George Orwell novel "1984" warned that the one who controls the language controls the mind. Now, the preferred term for immigrants is newcomers. Terrorists must be politely called freedom fighters. The designations Before Christ (BC) and Anno Domini (AD) are now colloquially labeled Before Common Era (BCE) and Common Era (C). Also, books and films that do not adhere to the latest politically correct terms or messages are also canceled by our society. As mentioned previously, certain Dr. Seuss books are no longer published, while The *Adventures of Huckleberry Finn* is no longer read in many public schools. Even sports teams such as the Washington Redskins and the Cleveland Indians lost their names and logos. The Cultural Marxists believe that by neutralizing language, it will neutralize the mind. A mind without an original thought is an easy one to control.

Those that disagree with this new and ever-changing PC language of the Cultural Marxists are canceled. Opposition against the new Western vernacular is not allowed. Cultural Marxists like Rebecca Carroll wrote, "Fear lies at the heart of opposition to political correctness. People are afraid of the power that true equality can give the historically disenfranchised and afraid of having been wrong."

Carroll and other Culturist Marxists alike are correct that "fear lies at the heart of opposition." However, it certainly is not the fear to which Carroll miscategorized. The fear is being canceled by the Marxist left and by the institutes that they have infected. All those who do not adhere to the constantly changing PC vocabulary can potentially become a pariah in their work, in their family, and in their community. Failure to conform is not an option, and many are too frightened to speak up against such blatant censorship as a result.

A Free Speech and Tolerance survey conducted by the Cato Institute concluded that "71% of Americans believe that political correctness has silenced important discussions our society needs to have." A different survey from the same institute showed that 62% of Americans say that the political climate of today prevents them from voicing what they believe.

The fear is justified. Those that dissent are labeled with a psychiatric or sort of personality disorder and fear losing their entire livelihood. Plus, they are under public scrutiny and negatively labeled as such things as a nativist, xenophobes, or transphobes—as preached by Theodore Adorno.

A popular term the Cultural Marxists also use to stigmatize those that disagree with them is "fascist." The irony is that most of them have no clue what a fascist is or why they use the term so flagrantly and ignorantly. *Wikipedia* describes fascism as "an ultra-nationalistic political etiology and movement characterized by a dictatorial leader, centralized autocracy, militarism, forcible suppression of opposition, belief in a natural social hierarchy, subordination of individual interests for the perceived good of the nation and race, and strong regimentation of society and the economy." When one thinks of a fascist, Adolf Hitler and Benito Mussolini come to mind.

However, this definition of a fascist more suitably describes the Cultural Marxists rather than those that they are seeking to slander. Are they not the ones suppressing opposition, subordinating their interests to a perceived goal, believing in a natural social hierarchy, and having an extremely dogmatic political etiology? It was not the conservative group Turning Point USA oppressing free speech at the UC Berkley event. It was not the Christian group Crusaders for Christ shouting down Alex Marlow on stage. It also was not the American Family Association destroying police property in Ferguson, Missouri.

The reason why the Cultural Marxists of today unknowingly label all opposition as fascists directly relate back to the Frankfurt School and Theodor Adorno's 1950 book, "The Authoritarian Personality." The goal of this book was to help identify someone as having an "authoritarian personality," as identified by Adorno. He believed these types of people held the exact traits opposite to what he was looking for in a modern revolutionary who would bring down capitalism and all of Western society. The scale he invented to grade this type of personality was called the F-Scale, where "F" stood for fascist.

The higher number you totaled on the score, the more

authoritarian or fascist you were considered by his perceived standards. The test consisted of 30 personality-oriented questions encompassing nine different personality variables. People who adhered to middle-class values and obeyed law and order were at the top of the list. In the end, the scale was never validated, and its purpose proved debatable at best. Plus, the test never really identified a person possessing true fascist beliefs as intended. It did, however, give an idea of how conservative the beliefs a person held.

Though modern-day Cultural Marxists believe that they are calling a person Hitler when labeling them as a fascist, what they are pointing out unknowingly is that the person actually holds conservative values. So faith in God, country, and law and order is actually fascist, according to Theodor Adorno's F-Scale.

How ironically ignorant.

Another method by which Cultural Marxists shut down free speech and independent thought is through a concept called sensitivity training. Though the concept seems like a modern creation, it was also the brainchild of Theodor Adorno. The *Encyclopedia Britannica* defines sensitivity training as a "psychological technique in which intensive group discussion and interaction are used to increase individual awareness of self and others."

At its surface, the concept seems like a productive endeavor. Jesus said in Luke 6:31, "Do to others as you would have them do to you." The idea of sensitivity training would appear to adopt this golden rule. However, this concept was never meant to be productive. Instead, just like Critical Race Theory and Critical Theory, the practice's intent has always been nefarious and destructive in nature. Sensitivity training, by its nature, means brainwashing. It is meant to destroy a person's values and sense of self-worth. It is also designed to discredit what a person feels is factual and create a sense of confusion and vulnerability. It is during this weakened state that a new sense of worth, moral standards, and way of thinking can be drilled into a person.

A prime example is how the Chinese used their form of sensitivity training for the POW in North Korea. Instead of physical torture, their goal was that of mind control. Their tactics were simple. They taught the prisoners about the positives of communism and the negatives of American culture and capitalism. The prisoners were also asked to comply with simple tasks, such as repeating statements like, "America is not perfect," or, "In a communist country, employment is not a problem." They were also asked to write these statements down on paper.

Through repetition of techniques such as this, psychiatrists uncovered that the Chinese were able to manipulate the POWs' minds. These soldiers were regrettably more apt to turn in fellow prisoners and had more empathy toward the communists.

Corporate America, the media, and the American education system have been implementing their own form of sensitivity training for years throughout the country. By repeating certain messages, employing certain programs, and adhering to the same Marxist doctrines, the Cultural Marxists' messages have permeated into the subconscious mind of America and all of Western culture.

As a result of this manipulated truth and constant Marxist messaging, attitudes in the country and throughout the West have changed. More Americans believe socialism and communism are positive despite the disastrous economic conditions in Venezuela and the horrors of the 20th century staring us right in the face. Also, more people believe that they are the victims and that their plight in this world is due solely to external factors while neglecting all internal responsibilities. We are a society apt to point the finger at others for the problems in our lives as opposed to pointing them at ourselves. Consequently, we are now questioning our government, religions, political institutions, morals, and values like never before.

The goal of the Cultural Marxists is coming to full fruition before our eyes. If we do not wake up now, we could find this country fundamentally changed for the worse.

CHAPTER 8
BLACK LIVES MATTER

To deny racial tensions in America would be to deny history itself. Black distrust of America certainly has a firm foundation dating back hundreds of years. Though the issue began with slavery, the abolition of this institution by former President Lincoln through the Emancipation Proclamation did not solve the problem. After the formal institution of slavery ended, an era of segregation began in the country.

In the former Confederate States of America, Black Laws or Black Codes were enacted. Some examples, as referenced by The American Social History Project, include:

- *Any person who is able to work is not allowed to wander or stroll about leisurely. Such people will be deemed vagrants and be arrested. Anyone can arrest a vagrant. Landowners or other people with a source of income are not subject to vagrancy laws (Georgia).*
- *No person of color can testify against a white person in court, unless the white person agrees to it (North Carolina).*
- *It is a felony crime for any person of color to marry a white person; white people may not marry freedmen or other people of color. Any person who commits this crime will be sentenced to*

life in prison (Mississippi).

- *Only white men can serve on juries, hold office, and vote in any state, county, or municipal election (Texas).*
- *No colored persons have the right to vote, hold office or sit on juries in this state.*

The problem with these laws was that black people would be rounded up in the middle of the street and arrested with little or no just cause. They were then forced to work against their will and leased to private companies that put them to hard labor in such places as coal mines, turpentine factories, and lumber camps without pay. Blacks effectively became indentured servants, which only proved to be a new form of slavery.

This time also saw the rise of the Ku Klux Klan. This white supremacist group rallied against not only black Americans but also Jews, Catholics, and Latinos, among other racial minorities. Their original goal was to disenfranchise the newly freed black slaves and intimidate them through violence, harassment, and indiscriminate force. The Klan's popularity and power waned by the late 19th century only to regain momentum in the early 20th century, boasting over four million members nationally. Their nighttime burning of the crosses and white hoods became their symbols of oppression and fear.

Jim Crow Laws were also established between the years 1874 and 1975. These laws were theoretically created to give black Americans a "separate but equal" status. In reality, the laws led to inferior treatment and standards while creating a racial hierarchy throughout the country. The laws required blacks to attend separate schools and churches, use separate "colored" bathrooms and water fountains, eat in separate locations in a restaurant, and sit in the rear of the bus, among other racial restrictions. After the US Supreme Court upheld the Jim Crow Laws in Plessy v. Ferguson (1896), it marked the beginning of a 58-year period where these laws were largely unchallenged.

It was not until civil rights lawyer Thurgood Marshall won several key victories in the US Supreme Court, beginning in 1946, that the Jim Crow Laws began to finally unravel. Marshall's victories in the court culminated with his ultimate victory in 1954 in the case Brown vs. the Board of Education. This success effectively ended the separate but equal doctrine set forth by Plessy vs. Fergusson and abolished the Jim Crow Laws. After winning 29 of the 32 civil rights cases he brought before the Supreme Court, Marshal ultimately went on to be the first black US Supreme court justice, serving from 1967 to 1991.

Redlining also served as a means to segregate the black community and deter racial integration. In the 1930s, the US government classified different neighborhoods according to how safe it was to issue them loans. Each area was color-coded to designate its monetary risk. Green meant "best," blue meant "still desirable," yellow meant "definitely declining," and red meant "hazardous."

The predominantly black neighborhoods on these maps were typically labeled red, essentially discouraging banks from loaning US citizens residing in these areas from getting loans needed to buy or renovate a house. Therefore, those living in a red-colored neighborhood were colloquially "redlined" from getting any bank loans. It was not until 1968, with the Fair Lending Act, and in 1977 with the Community Reinvestment Act, that the flagrant and discriminatory use of redlining came to an end.

One large black eye on the medical community was what is remembered as the "Tuskegee experiment." Originally labeled the "Tuskegee Study of Untreated Syphilis in the Negro Male," the experiment was conducted by the Center for Disease Control and the United States Public Health Services to monitor the natural progression of syphilis in 399 black men. The experiment began in 1932 in Alabama with the help of the predominantly black institution, Tuskegee University.

The study was conducted without informed consent and without any subjects' knowledge of their disease or the purpose of the experiment. Not only were the participants unaware that they had syphilis, but they were also banned from any effective treatment for the disease, despite penicillin becoming a proven therapy for it in 1943. During this time, some of the study participants spread the disease, passed it to their children via their mates, and suffered from the ravages of this illness. It was not until 1972 that the study finally ended. The stigma of this experiment lasts until this day. Many black Americans still remain skeptical of the entire medical community and do not obtain proper medical care as a result.

A more recent insult to the black community was a law sponsored by Senator Biden, now President Biden, and signed under then-President Bill Clinton in 1994, known as The Violent Crime Control and Law Enforcement Act, or Crime Bill for short. Meant to "get tough on crime," it decimated the inner-city neighborhoods. Instead of reducing crime, it proved only to increase incarceration rates and the overall prison population. Its sole mandate was that of punishment and ignored rehabilitation.

The Crime Bill had dogmatic elements in it, like the "three strike provision," whereby repeat criminal offenders were given life sentences. It also created new laws that mandated jail time if broken and authorized stiffer criminal penalties. For example, a mandatory extra ten years was added to a sentence if a person committed a crime within a thousand feet of a school.

In the end, this bill ultimately decimated the inner-city population. It took fathers out of the house, destroyed families, and created even more poverty. Instead of preventing crime, it created even more of it, along with increased social and economic problems for inner-city populations.

It also created a massive incarceration boom. According to the Department of Justice, under President Bill Clinton, the U.S. prison population swelled to nearly two million people, with blacks as the majority. The incarceration for blacks increased from about 3,000 per 100,000 to 3,620 per 100,000 during this time.

Out of this long history of discontentment, the Black Lives Matter movement ultimately emerged, whereby the black community said to both America and the rest of the world that they count and that their lives actually mattered. It was originally meant as means for them to stand up for themselves and voice that they are tired of feeling marginalized and victimized by society.

However, the problem with this movement began before it even started and intensified after being hijacked by the Cultural Marxist wing of the Democratic Party. Though intended to help the black community, the movement became a means of Marxist propaganda and was ultimately overrun with corruption. Plus, the black community, which the organization was supposed to help, never benefited monetarily from its fundraising.

The lie that sparked the proverbial racial keg that had been brewing in America and fueled by identity politics was the Treyvon Martin incident. The story made national headlines in 2012 when a 911 call was televised on NBC's *Today Show.* The show aired the 911 dispatcher's call from George Zimmerman, the man who shot Martin.

It was broadcasted as follows, "This guy looks like he's up

to no good. He looks black."

The 911 call initially met the Cultural Marxist narrative perfectly. Innocent black teen murdered by a racist white man. The oppressor, a white man, killed a member of a marginalized/victimized group, a black teen. It was the exact type of story they sought out and tried to exploit. This precise narrative played out over and over again across the airways, TV, newspapers, magazines, and talk shows and was drilled into the minds of every American across the country. You could not turn on the news without seeing something about Trayvon Martin.

The problem with this narrative was that it was a lie. First of all, Zimmerman turned out to be Hispanic. Secondly, his call 911 call was not racially motivated. Instead of what *The Today Show* aired, the actual conversation went as follows:

- **Zimmerman:** *This guy looks like he's up to no good. Or he's on drugs or something. It's raining, and he's just walking around, looking about.*
- **Dispatcher:** *OK, and this guy—is he black, white, or Hispanic?*
- **Zimmerman:** *He looks black.*

There was no bigoted call to 911. *The Today Show* selectively edited the story in order to create a racial melee out of it. In addition, the shooting was deemed a matter of self-defense. An eyewitness to the event recalled seeing a black male "wearing a dark-colored hoodie on top of a white or Hispanic male who was yelling for help." And that he "was mounted on the white or Hispanic male and throwing punches MMA-style (mixed martial arts)." After calling 911, he heard a "pop" and saw Martin on the grass.

Despite the truth coming out, the original narrative, as

told by *The Today Show*, still remains true to many Americans. This scenario is a prime example of how Cultural Marxists view truth as arbitrary. As long as the narrative achieves its desired outcome, it is true to them. The outcome here was to create racial unrest, while in Fergusson, the objective was the overthrow the stability of law and order.

If *The Today's Show's* story was an isolated event, one may believe that it could be a case of poor journalism. However, these false narratives reported by the media have become commonplace. The Duke lacrosse rape scandal, the Nicholas Sandman taunting of an elderly native American event, the Jussie Smollett lie, and the Rachel Richardson Duke/BYU racial slur incident are some prime examples of how the Cultural Marxists attempt to influence America through lies and deception.

Out of this media-fueled racial chaos, the Black Lives Matter organization arose. Though created originally with positive intent, the Cultural Marxists hijacked the group. From the start, their agenda was like a page taken right out of the Frankfurt School. Plus, their logo did not hide their true intent.

Communist Fist

Black Lives Matter Fist

`

The goal of the Cultural Marxists' involvement with BLM was to break down Western society under the guise of racism. There was absolutely no denying racism existed. However, their aim was to utilize this tension in order to disrupt law and order and create massive political and civil unrest.

Real problems remain within the black communities. Crime, illegal drugs, poor schools, black-on-black violence, lack of meaningful industry, and poverty are just a start. Instead of tackling these pressing issues, BLM took an immediate Cultural Marxist stance and embraced a Frankfurt School agenda.

BLM's first demand was to defund and abolish the police. Instead of taking a more moderate position, such as investigating the police and their policies, they demanded that this Western institution be torn down. As critical theory demands, be critical of everything and everyone within the justice system. Because BLM believed "police were born out of slave patrols" and that is an "institution built upon white supremacy," it was beyond reform and needed to be dismantled (*Blacklivesmatter.com*).

In certain areas around the country, this cop-free "utopia" came to fruition. The Capital Hill Organized Protest (CHOP) and later the Capitol Hill Autonomous Zone (CHAZ) in Seattle, Washington, are prime examples. Looting, property damage, increased crime rates, and gang rule became the norm in these areas. It was the perfect grounds for chaos whereby a revolution could take place. Though small scale, one could imagine what would have happened if these areas spread throughout the country.

Besides insisting that the police be defunded, BLM's other demands were just as radical and could be found on their webpage, *blacklivesmatter.com/what-we-believe*. Though this page was eventually taken down, the internet has a way of never forgetting.

BLM called for the disruption of "the Western-prescribed nuclear family structure requirement by supporting each other as extended families and 'villages.'" As Marx himself elaborates, "Abolition of the family! On what foundation is the present family, the bourgeois family, based? On capital, on private gain. In its completely developed form, this family exists only among the bourgeoisie."

Instead of parents being responsible for their children, BLM joined the Cultural Marxists' call for the state, or "village," to raise the next generation. If the state raises the child, the state, instead of the family, could instill its own set of morals and beliefs in today's youths. They could coddle them from the time they are born until the time they die, from crib to coffin. It is the exact formula for brainwashing the next generation so thoroughly that they cannot discern fact from fiction. One need not look further than North Korea to see how absolutely effective this method can be. In the end, without a stable nuclear family, Western society cannot exist.

BLM goes on further to attack heterosexuality. They want to "dismantle cis-gender privilege and uplift black trans folk." They also want to free themselves "from the tight grip of heteronormative thinking, or rather, the belief that all in the world are heterosexual." The Cultural Marxist message is simple. The patriarchal society of today is run by white, cis-gender males in stable relationships who raise their own children are the oppressors, while everyone else not in this category are the marginalized and victims in society.

A movement to end racial injustice, constructively reform the criminal justice system, and help Black America as a whole would certainly have been a noble one. However,

BLM has grossly fallen short on all measures. Not only had BLM failed to act upon the true needs of the black communities, but they had also been plagued by internal scandals and inefficiency.

In 2020, BLM Global Network raised 90 million dollars in funds. The outpouring of giving was a true testament to the generosity and commitment to end racism by many Americans. The belief was this money would help Black America and further the cause for racial equality in the country.

In 2020, BLM Global Network wanted to have a tax-exempt status. As a result, they needed to file an IRS Form 900 to make public their accounting practices. It was the first time the organization was made publicly responsible for outlining where the donations given to them were being utilized.

Instead of directly helping Black America, Form 900, unfortunately, revealed that the group it was helping out most was themselves. A total of 60 million dollars was spent by the organization in the fiscal year 2020-2021, leaving them with 42 million dollars of remaining assets. Thirty-two million dollars went directly into stocks that benefited only the national organization. Close to two more million dollars went to kickbacks benefiting BLM co-founder Patrisse Cullors' family. $970,000 went to Trap Heals LLC, a company founded by the father of Cullors' child, Damon Turner, and another $840,000 went to a security firm, Cullors Protection LLC, run by Cullors' brother, Paul Cullors. Another 8.4 million dollars went to operating expenses. However, the form did not break down what these expenses were and did not delineate how they were spent.

Another large expenditure went to a mansion that BLM Global Network bought for themselves. The property cost close to 6 million dollars and was located in an affluent Los Angeles neighborhood. It boasted seven bedrooms, seven bathrooms, a sound stage, a music studio, several fireplaces, a pool, a bungalow, and a two-bedroom guest house. The home also once welcomed such well-known guests as Humphrey Bogart and Marilyn Monroe.

If BLM was not forced to disclose this mansion in their IRS filings, would they have even let the world know how they were using their donations? Though they claim yes, the story of how they purchased the home would tell a different story. The house was initially purchased by Patrisse Cullors' business associate, Dyane Pascall, using BLM funds. As the Intelligencer explains, "Pascall is the financial manager for Janaya and Patrisse Consulting, an LLC run by Cullors and her spouse, Janaya Khan. Pascall is also the chief financial officer for Trap Heals, a nonprofit led by Damon Turner, the father of Cullors' only child." These business associations run deep and get more convoluted the more you research them.

The house was then transferred by the law firm Perkins Coie to an LLC located in Delaware. The move was meant to hide the ownership of the property. BLM Global Network leaders such as Cullors then assumed responsibility for the mansion and began using it as they pleased. Known as "The Campus," this property was a far cry from how hard-working Americans thought their well-intentioned donations would be spent.

Another executive at the BLM Global Network, Shalomyah Bowers, was accused of siphoning off ten million dollars from BLM donations directly into his own business, Bowers Consulting Firm. This accusation came directly from private BLM chapters across the country through an organization they formed called BLM Grassroots. Ironically, Bowers was directly hired by Patrisse

Cullors.

The lawsuit against Bowers also revealed that BLM Global Network was created by Cullors as "an administrative organization to raise funds to provide financial support for local-level community efforts of BLM Grassroots."

The IRS Form 900 proved that the BLM Global Foundation had failed miserably in its mission statement. From misappropriation of funds to outright theft, the organization had perverted its philanthropic cause into one of decadence, dishonesty, and corruption.

However, in the eyes of the Cultural Marxist movement, it remains a massive success. As long as they promote the Marxist cause, the truth that it is a corrupt organization squandering the generosity of others is not important. Because BLM promotes the abolition of a nuclear family, the dismantling of all law enforcement, and the advancement of non-heterosexual lifestyles, it remains a poster child of the Cultural Marxist movement.

The facts about the organization are blatantly obvious. However, the media, which has been highly infiltrated by the Cultural Marxist movement, turn a blind eye to them. Truthful reporting by the media would have called for the BLM Global Foundation to cease further activities and insisted that its tax-exempt status be revoked. If this were a Christian or conservative group, it would be headline news all day and all night. The selective reporting which ignited the movement is also saving it from its own self-destruction.

☐

CHAPTER 9
SEXUAL REVOLUTION

The work of Herbert Marcuse from the Frankfurt School was the foundation behind the 1960s sexual revolution. Combining both Marxist beliefs and Freudian psychoanalysis, his 1955 book, "Eros and Civilization," condemns all restrictions on sexual behavior. The book also denounces traditional sexual morals and Judeo-Christian sexual values.

Marcuse believed that liberating humans' erotic side was the only way to escape the modern industrial society. He went on to state that people are meant to be an instrument of pleasure and not that of labor. Marcuse's goal was to destroy the patriarchal family and the belief in a traditional, monogamous relationship. His work also promoted 'taboo' practices of the day, such as homosexuality and pedophilia, and he wanted to normalize them. Despite the disastrous implementation of these beliefs in Hungary by his predecessor, György Lukács, Marcuse stood by his work.

"Eros and Civilization" became the blueprint for America's sexual revolution of the 1960s. As *Wikipedia* defines it, the sexual revolution "was a social and cultural movement that resulted in liberalized attitudes toward sex and morality. In the 1960s, social norms were changing as sex became more widely discussed in society."

The ideas of free sex, LSD, marijuana, and pornography started to become accepted by American society during this time. The music of the day reflected these new trends. Singers like Janis Joplin, Bob Dillon, and Grace Slick spoke to the youth of America. This time also marked the rise in feminism and the gay rights movement. America was turning away from the establishment and the war in Vietnam and embracing a new hedonistic counterculture.

It is these negative effects of the counterculture that still haunt our society today. All the free sex and liberalized sexual attitudes led to the rise of unwed births. The CDC National Center for Health and Statistics reported that the unwed births in 1960 of white babies rose from 3% to 22% today and from 20% in black babies to 70% currently. Divorce rates also continue to rise. According to the CDC, the divorce rate in 1964 was 24% and rose to 41% in 1999. There is also a rise in cohabitation and a decline in overall marriage in the United States. The Joint Economic Committee put out data that reported approximately 80% of households were made up of married couples in 1950, while in 2020, it dropped to 49%.

The rise in single mothers has led to a rise in poverty. A 2003 article in *The Heritage Foundation* reported that "children raised by never-married mothers were seven times more likely to be poor when compared to children raised in intact married families." The Pew Research Center reported that 3 in 10 solo mothers are living in poverty. *Family Structure and Children's Living Arrangements 2012* showed that 57.6% of black children, 31.2% of Hispanic children, and 20.7% of white children are in a living arrangement without their biological fathers.

There are also increased negative effects on children who live in single-parent households. *Social Science Research* reported, "Children in one-parent families also have lower grade point averages, lower college aspirations, and poorer attendance records. As adults, they have higher rates of divorce." In addition, *MedicineNet* related, "Children of single parents are more prone to various psychiatric illnesses, alcohol abuse, and suicide attempts than children from homes with two parents."

Also, like in Hungary during the time of György Lukács, our children are now being openly exposed to alternative lifestyles. Taxpayer dollars are currently being used to promote the LGBTQ agenda on such publicly-funded television channels as PBS. Recently, *Sesame Street* aired an episode where Billy Porter, a male Emmy and Tony-winning actor, was seen in drag wearing a dress. Also, in the newest animated Scooby-Doo movie, *Trick or Treat Scooby-Doo*, Velma Dinkley comes out as an openly gay character. Kellogg's released its "Together With Pride" cereal for kids, while the children's show *Blue's Clues* had a drag queen sing a song that celebrated LGBTQ identities. Even LEGO released a rainbow-colored set called "Everyone is Awesome" for Pride Month.

Today, our children are being inundated with sexual content from commercials, TV, movies, books, and in video games. It is confusing enough growing up, let alone being exposed to conflicting sexual messages. Certain studies and a book published by *The Heritage Foundation*, "The Harmful Effects of Early Sexual and Multiple Sexual Partners Among Women: Book of Notes," have shown that girls who engage in sexual behavior now at an earlier age can be prone to depressive disorders, violent behaviors, dating violence, and high-risk behaviors.

Sex and violence are also highly prevalent in video games played by children. Though showing porn to kids is taboo, the sexual content in them can be just as harmful. A study by *Clinical Pediatrics* revealed that such exposure to sexual content at a young age "was related to ever having had sex, coercive sex victimization, and attempted/completed rape" in youth between the ages of 14-21. Playing violent and over-sexualized video games has also been shown by the American Academy of Child & Adolescent Psychiatry to lead to "less time socializing with friends and family, poor social skills, time away from family time, schoolwork and other hobbies, lower grades, less reading, less exercise and becoming overweight, decreased sleep and poor-quality sleep, and aggressive thoughts and behaviors."

The sexual revolution also led to the rise in pornography and addiction to it. Though there were magazines such as *Playboy* that existed even before the 1960s revolution, pornography since that time has become more graphic and explicit in nature. Women have become more objectified, and intimacy in relations is becoming lost. As a result, psychologists blame pornography for adding to the increased rates of divorce.

The contraceptive pill also helped fuel the lack of intimacy in relationships. Without the fear of getting pregnant, women now had the luxury of having as many sexual partners as they wanted and without potential consequences. Without the fear of getting pregnant, they could pursue a career, hold off on getting married, and choose when the time is right for them to become a mother. Plus, if the pill didn't work, abortion was an acceptable and legal alternative to many in order to terminate the pregnancy.

What was meant to be "liberating" just for women turned out to be just as "liberating" for the opposite sex. Where was the man's responsibility in this new society? They also garnered the same freedoms, and it also allowed them the opportunity to defer commitment. They could also have relationships with as many women as they wanted without fearing unwanted pregnancies. An article in the *Wall Street Journal* by Louise Perry states, "Studies consistently find that following hookups, women are more likely than men to experience regret, low self-esteem and mental distress." As a result, relationships are becoming disposable commodities.

Another unintended result of the sexual revolution was shrinking family sizes. The U.S. Census Bureau, Historical Statistics of the United States, reported homes consisting of four or more people decreased from 40.2% in 1960 to 22.1% in 2019 and that the average US family consisted now of only 2.52 people. It is no surprise that loneliness in Americans is on the rise. Smaller families, increased divorce rates, and the decline in the number of intact nuclear families have all aided in this problem. A study completed by the Harvard Graduate School of Education noted that 36% of Americans are now experiencing serious loneliness. It also reported that "61% of young people aged 18-25 and 51% of mothers with young children reported these miserable degrees of loneliness."

This loneliness and societal dysfunction are the exact goals the Frankfurt School and especially Herbert Marcuse hoped to achieve. Unhappiness is the seed of revolution, and that seed was planted in the 1960s sexual revolution. Marcuse understood that social change was necessary to create the downstream economic transformation they desired. The ends justify the means to the Cultural Marxists. If it means destroying stable nuclear families, morality, and peoples' lives, it is justified.

CHAPTER 10
RULES FOR RADICALS

No other person has learned to implement the beliefs of the Cultural Marxists as effectively and ruthlessly as the famed American Communist Saul Alinsky. He was known as a political organizer and had garnered many well-known disciples around the country. Some of the noblest of these include Cesar Chavez, Hillary Clinton, Bill Ayers, and Bernardine Dohrn. Later followers included the likes of former President Obama and Congresswomen Alexandria Ocasio-Cortez. In fact, Hillary Clinton's 1969 college thesis was on Saul Alinsky.

Alinsky considered himself a political organizer and utilized the idea of victimhood to incite the masses. Through tactics that were meant to utterly destroy his opponents through intimidation, violence, humiliation, and economic despair, he was relentless in his cause. Alinsky was, at heart, a Satanist and a man without morals who believed the ends always justified the means. In fact, he wrote:

"Lest we forget at least an over-the-shoulder acknowledgment to the very first radical: from all our legends, mythology, and history (and who is to know where mythology leaves off and history begins — or which is which), the first radical known to man who rebelled against the establishment and did it so effectively that he at least won his own kingdom — Lucifer."

Alinsky's tactics were outlined in his book, "Rules for Radicals," from which the above quotation was taken. This handbook outlines how to implement these tactics. In summary, there were 13 different "rules" or guidelines to follow in order to achieve a desired political goal:

1. "Power is not only what you have, but what the enemy thinks you have."

The illusion of power is more important than actual power. Act like you have more power and influence than you do. It will make you seem stronger and more intimidating.

2. "Never go outside the expertise of your people."

Don't address topics beyond the knowledge of your members. Instead, work on emotions and not facts or reason.

3. "Whenever possible, go outside the expertise of the enemy."

It is an effective means of distraction. Even if irrelevant facts are used, it can confuse the opponent, and you can take advantage of the situation.

4. "Make the enemy live up to its own book of rules."

Point out when the opposition slips in their morality and hold them accountable for the hypocrisy. However, disregard your own hypocrisy and make no mention of it.

5. "Ridicule is man's most potent weapon."

Use character assassination to demoralize and defeat enemies. Be relentless with this tactic.

6. "A good tactic is one your people enjoy."

It is easier to attract members if they are doing something that they enjoy doing. Do not bore them.

7. "A tactic that drags on too long becomes a drag."
Again, don't bore your members. They will grow tired and lose interest in the movement.

8. "Keep the pressure on. Never let up."
Ruthlessly keep pressure on the opposition. The quantity of the pressure, not quality, is most important.

9. "The threat is usually more terrifying than the thing itself."
Threats and intimidation are effective means to bring your opposition to submission.

10. "The major premise for tactics is the development of operations that will maintain a constant pressure upon the opposition."
The goal is to provoke a response from your opponent and then play the innocent victim as a result.

11. "If you push a negative hard enough, it will push through and become a positive."
Violence can win public support because the public sympathizes with the underdog.

12. "The price of a successful attack is a constructive alternative. "
Sometimes it is necessary to agree to a compromised, short-term solution. However, continue a constant offensive to achieve long-term goals.

13. "Pick the target, freeze it, personalize it, and polarize it."
Cut off the support network and isolate the opponent. There will be no sympathy. Go after people and not the institution they represent. People are easier targets and hurt much faster than institutions. Attack their friends, businesses, and families. Completely isolate the opponent.

Alinsky believed that "the first step to community organization is community disorganization. The disruption of the present organization is the first step toward community organization. Present arrangements must be disorganized if they are to be displaced by new patterns... All change means disorganization of the old and organization of the new."

His tactics were meant to destroy. True compromise, building trust, and working together were never options. There were no other choices other than his own, and he wanted to destroy anyone or anything that stood in front of him.

The unethical nature of his tactics was outlined in a chapter titled *Of Means and Ends*:

1. One's concern with the ethics of means and ends varies inversely with one's personal interest in the issue.
2. The judgment of the ethics of means is dependent upon the political position of those sitting in judgment.
3. In war, the end justifies almost any means.
4. Judgment must be made in the context of the times in which the action occurred and not from any other chronological vantage point.
5. Concern with ethics increases with the number of means available and vice versa.
6. The less important the end to be desired, the more one can afford to engage in ethical evaluations of means.
7. The ethics of means and ends is that generally success or failure is a mighty determinant of ethics.
8. The morality of a means depends upon whether the means is being employed at a time of imminent defeat or imminent victory.
9. Any effective means is automatically judged by the

opposition as being unethical.

10. You do what you can with what you have and clothe it with moral garments.
11. Goals must be phrased in general terms like "Liberty, Equality, Fraternity," "Of the Common Welfare," "Pursuit of Happiness," or "Bread and Peace."

Saul Alinsky is considered the father of the modern leftist movement. He is a man without morals or ethics who revels in the evils of Satan. His disciples now are many and have garnered full control of the new Democratic Party. With a Cultural Marxist agenda and tactics passed on to them from Alinsky, the political left has become ruthless in its grab for power and total control of American politics and each of our lives.

Utilizing Alinsky's tactics, the political left has mercilessly attacked and attempted to destroy former President Trump. Truth, along with the rules of law and order, is inconsequential to them. They have attempted to destroy the former president's life through two fabricated impeachment trials, Russiagate, the lawsuit by NY Attorney General for real estate fraud, the unconstitutional raid on Mar-a-Lago, and the constant character and personal attacks that have become relentless.

Alinsky's "Rules for Radicals" tactics are on full display with the left's quest to bring down Trump. The former president has been relentlessly (#10) ridiculed, (#5) intimidated, (#9) and called every name possible. They have attempted to isolate (#13) him from his family, friends, and political allies while endeavoring to destroy him financially in the process. Their method of attack constantly changes (#7), and they enjoy (#6) keeping him on the constant defensive.

These are the beliefs of the Cultural Marxists and the methods through which they pursue their goals. There is no political debate or room for compromise. Step in their way, and they will destroy you and everything and everyone you love. The ends to them justify the means. Do not get in their way, or you will pay the price.

Welcome to America!

Chapter 11
How to beat the Cultural Marxists

We are currently in a cultural war, a war that the Cultural Marxists are winning by the day. As they are now at the helm of America's mass media juggernaut, have infiltrated the education system, and have taken control of many politicians, it seems like an unwinnable battle. Plus, the Cultural Marxists are ruthless in their tactics and use a scorched-earth policy to destroy their opponents and all that they cherish. With tactics taken directly from Saul Alinsky, most Americans remain silent in fear of ostracization, humiliation, and loss of livelihood.

The problem is that what most Americans and those of Western society are doing is that they are falling for the first rule in Alinsky's "Rules for Radicals": "Power is not only what you have, but what the enemy thinks you have." A Gallup poll showed that 37% of Americans described their political views as moderate, 36% as conservative, and 25% as liberal. Even though the Cultural Marxists want you to believe that they are the majority and that anyone who disagrees with them is an outlier, they are actually in the minority. America is a much more moderate and conservative country than it is liberal. The numbers are clearly not on the Cultural Marxist's side.

The cost of losing this cultural war is the collapse of

Western civilization. And remember, there is no communist or socialist paradise waiting for us in the end. As the once-prosperous Venezuela clearly illustrates, only poverty, crime, and despair loom on the horizon. This is the reason why winning this cultural war is so important. We are not only saving our current generation but many future generations to come. Just think of where the world would be now if it did not stand up to the Nazi onslaught. How would our lives be? Just like the "greatest generation," we must stand up for our country before there is no country left to stand up for.

The Cultural Marxists want it to appear as if they hold the moral high ground and that those who adhere to the idea of a traditional nuclear family, believe in God, or love America are the outcasts. With terms like xenophobe, homophobe, colonist, and racist, they attempt to shut down all oppositional content. No longer do the Cultural Marxists want to portray themselves as extremists. They want everyone else to believe that they are the minority, and they are proverbial radicals for their belief in such antiquated values.

If the Cultural Marxists are ever going to be defeated, they need to be confronted from new angles and with new strategies. If they want to create a perception that all Americans with moderate or conservative views are to be considered social pariahs or outcasts, a "New Rules for Radicals" needs to be created in order to beat the Cultural Marxists at their own game.

Where do we start, and what are these "new rules" to take back our country?

1. In order to defeat the Cultural Marxists, you must first understand them. In Sun Tzu's "Art of War," he writes, "If you know the enemy and know

yourself, you need not fear the result of a hundred battles. If you know yourself but not the enemy, for every victory gained, you will also suffer a defeat. If you know neither the enemy nor yourself, you will succumb in every battle." What the late, great Chinese general is telling us is that we have to truly know the Cultural Marxists, their beliefs, strategies, weaknesses, and faults. You cannot beat them unless you understand them. The more knowledge you gain about the Cultural Marxists' history, goals, tactics, and methods of action, the easier it will be to win the cultural war.

See the Cultural Marxists as who they really are and know that their goal is one of destruction. Though they attempt to disguise their methods under the pretext of helping the disenfranchised, ending racism, and freeing the world of "hate speech," their motives are not genuine. They are playing on the goodwill of many Americans so that they will be blinded from what is really happening. It's like a magician who does a sleight-of-hand trick. Their goal is to create an illusion of what they want you to believe while deliberating hiding the truth through trickery and misdirection.

2. There is power in numbers. Remember, the Cultural Marxists are the minority. As a majority, we have the power to cancel the "cancelers." If Hollywood is dumping out to the public another PC, incorrect, historical rewrite, such as "The Women King," boycott their movies. Remember, we live in a capitalist society that utilizes the law of supply and demand. If the products being produced by Hollywood are subpar, don't purchase them. The end result will be better movies, or the entire film industry will go financially bankrupt. If Gillette is

putting out commercials depicting men as being driven by "toxic masculinity," don't buy their shaving products or other goods. Instead, purchase your products from The Dollar Shave Club.

What is more important is that we must have a method to mobilize our numbers. Just as the political left mobilizes the mainstream media to rally for their latest cause, we must do the same. There has to be a method whereby a message spreads to all moderates and conservatives across the country to support in numbers a pro-American cause or boycott a woke product.

3. Shun those companies that use the policies and vocabulary of the Cultural Marxists. Don't do business with them and encourage others to do the same. There are always different options to choose from. Whether it be food, a car, a form of entertainment, or simply a household necessity, a variety of other possibilities exist. The power of the purse goes a long way.

4. People who love America and Western values should strive to be on the board of directors of these large and even small companies. Why have so many of these corporations, such as Google, Facebook, Gillette, and Disney, been inundated with woke Cultural Marxists who populate their boards? Change has to come from within. The right people need to hold these positions of power so that an America-first agenda can be pursued and not one based upon Cultural Marxists' values.

5. Set up alternative businesses based upon "Western" values or create companies that are completely apolitical in nature. Complementary businesses not adhering to the latest Cultural Marxist fad are needed to compete against the status quo. If just the

conservatives who live in America switched to them, there would be a 36% shift in the market. Imagine Google or Facebook losing 36% of their business. It would be a financial nightmare. Businesses would be forced to flee from the Cultural Marxist dogma out of fear of bankruptcy. Money talks. Their stocks would plummet. Plus, if alternative businesses already exist, support them instead. Why must Google always be the go-to search engine? The Cultural Marxists believe that economics is downstream from culture. However, this theory is a falsehood. Let's see how the culture of these Cultural Marxist-adherent businesses would be if their economic bottom line changed. I doubt they would be mandating sensitivity training.

6. Elect school board representatives with more conservative values. Those pushing Cultural Marxist agendas have no place in deciding what our public school children should learn. If more America-loving people were on the school boards, such issues as Critical Race Theory would not even be a topic of conversation. The proper education of America's youth would be their top priority instead of attempting to create a nationwide Cultural Marxist indoctrination center.

7. Private schools are also an option. If the financial resources are available, send your child to a private or religious school if necessary. There, they would not be subjected to or influenced by Cultural Marxist doctrine or be forced to adhere to the new vocabulary of the left.

8. If possible, consider homeschooling. The number of homeschoolers continues to grow in America and has become more popular. Under these

circumstances, parents would have direct supervision of what their child was exposed to and what they would learn. Plus, the child would no longer be subject to group learning. They could go at their own pace and learn in a caring environment. In addition, any special needs or interests could be addressed directly and in a more personal and less judgmental environment.

9. Send a louder message to the public. Remember, the Cultural Marxists and liberals are a minority in the country. Why are their small number of voices monopolizing the topics of conversation? People who love America, God, and Western civilization should speak out. Their voices need to be heard. They are the majority. However, many conservatives and even moderates are afraid to express their minds for fear of ridicule and possible persecution. If more people were open about their beliefs and made them public, a new, positive, and pro-American message would be heard around the country.

10. Force mass media to change their message. Remember, conservatives and moderates are the vast majority. We do not have to stand any longer for Cultural Marxist narratives being force-fed to us on a daily basis. Unplug cable. Many media outlets would cease to exist without cable network subsidies. As CNN and MSNBC viewers continue to dwindle, without their checks from the cable companies, they would be unable to operate financially. If unplugging from cable is not an option, ask the cable company to remove certain channels like CNN from your subscription so you're not forced to pay for them.

Also, seek out alternative media outlets like *Newsmax* or *Breitbart*. The competition will also eventually force the establishment media to change in order to accommodate the needs of the public. There are excellent alternative media outlets available. Change your viewing habits.

11. Don't attempt to add logic to an illogical conversation. The goal of the Cultural Marxists is not to debate actual facts or have a meaningful conversation about a particular problem. Their aim is to force you into completely adhering to their will. Through misinformation, harassment, and force, the Cultural Marxists want to muscle themselves to victory. Trying to reason with them or attempting to bring meaningful facts and statistics to the conversation will prove only to be frustrating and time-consuming. It is like using all your energy to rock in a rocking chair. In the end, you have gone nowhere.

When confronted with the illogic of the Cultural Marxists, either completely dismiss yourself from the conversation or change the subject matter at hand. Their aim is to provoke a response. If you dismiss them and their argument, you have saved yourself a headache and did not grant the Cultural Marxist an opportunity to provoke a response. Also, by changing the subject on most Cultural Marxists, they will be unable to respond properly. With little original thought and armed with only insults, platitudes, and a few contrived talking points, they will be unable to react adequately. Instead of them provoking you, it will be them who are provoked.

12. Elect to office America-first representatives. There is power in the polls. Properly vetting the right candidate and getting out to vote for them in mass sends a powerful message to the local, state, and US governments. If enough of the right candidates get into office, the political policies will reflect a more

pro-American agenda. Plus, if a representative is doing a poor job, primary them out in the next election. Hold them accountable for their actions. If more representatives actually believed that they were beholden to their electorate, they would act more responsibly.

13. Live the American dream. There is nothing more that aggravates a Cultural Marxist than someone who wants to live the American dream. Get married. Have a bunch of kids. Go to church. Talk about God, Jesus, and how great America is. It will drive the Cultural Marxist crazy. There is nothing they hate more than a happy family full of kids with two parents in a monogamous relationship with great respect for God and country. Living and happily pursuing the American dream will give them nightmares.

What do the Cultural Marxists hope to actually produce if they win the cultural war and fundamentally change America and Western society? Are we looking at the "Great Reset"? Are we in for mass depopulation? Is global war the ultimate objective? Is the creation of a one-world government planned? Do they even know what they want? The authors do not have an answer. However, the result would be certain. Personal freedoms would be lost, economic prosperity would be a thing of the past, and a positive hope for a prosperous future would never be possible.

The cultural war against the Cultural Marxists is one that needs to be won for the preservation of not only America but also the entire Western civilization. We must act now before it is too late. Procrastination will only lead to loss. Hesitation will only prove to antagonize victory. If not for yourself, take a stand for your children and their children. Our veterans and military who fought the great wars of yonder did the same for this generation. Now it is your turn to return the favor to the next.

Selected Bibliography

1. Alinsky, Saul, *Rules for Radicals*, (Random House, 1971).
2. Bidden, Emma, "27 Celebrities Who Support the Republican Party," *Oprah Daily*, September 9, 2020.
3. Brennan, Dan "How Does Single Parenting Affect a Child?" *MedicineNet*, August 12, 2021.
4. Carroll, Rebecca, "Fear lies at the heart of opposition to 'political correctness'," The Guardian, October 22, 2015.
5. Elder, Alasdair, *The Red Trojan Horse*, (CreateSpace Independent Publishing Platform, 2017).
6. Fagen, Patrick, et al., "Increasing Marriage Would Dramatically Reduce Child Poverty," *The Heritage Foundation*, May 20, 2003.
7. Gross, Neil and Simmons, Salon. "The Social and Political Views of American College and University Professors," in *Professors and Their Politics*, ed. Neil Gross and Solon Simmons (Baltimore, 2014), pp. 19-49.
8. Ishizuka, Katie, Stephens, Ramón. "The Cat is Out of the Bag: Orientalism, Anti-Blackness, and White Supremacy in Dr. Seuss's Children's Books," *Research on Diversity in Youth Literature*: Vol. 1: Iss. 2, Article 4.
9. Marcuse, Herbert, Eros and Civilization, (Beacon Press, 1955).
10. McLanahan, Sara, "The Consequences of Single Motherhood." *The American Prospect*, December 19, 2021.
11. Rector, Robert, et al. The Harmful Effects of Early Sexual and Multiple Sexual Partners Among Women: Book of Notes, (*The Heritage Foundation*, 2003).

12. Sadler, "Single-Parent Families Cause Juvenile Crime," *Juvenile Crime: Opposing Viewpoints*, 1997, pp 62-66.

13. Schlichter, Kurt, "Don't Argue With Liberals – It Only Encourages Them," *Town Hall*, June 2, 2014.

14. Sheridan et al., "Changes in Suicidal Ingestion Among Preadolescent Children From 2000 to 2020," *JAMA Pediatrics*, Jun 1, 2022; 176(6):604-606.

15. Swan, Liz, "Safe Spaces Can Be Dangerous," Psychology Today, March 20, 2017.

16. Weissbourd, Richard, et al., "Loneliness in America How the Pandemic Has Deepened an Epidemic of Loneliness and What We Can Do About It," from Harvard Graduate School of Education's "Making Caring Common" project, February, 2021.

17. Ybarra, Michele, et al., "Sexual media exposure, sexual behavior, and sexual violence victimization in adolescence," *Clinical Pediatrics*, 2014 Nov; 53(13): 1239-47.

18. Youngmin Sun and Yuanzhang Li, "Parents' Marital Disruption and Its Uneven Effect on Children's Academic Performance- A Simulation Model," *Social Science Research* 37, (2008): 456.

ABOUT THE AUTHOR
DARYL M. BROOKS

Daryl M. Brooks is a former three times U.S. Senate/Congressman candidate. On a historical note, he is the first African American from Trenton, NJ to run for Congress. Also, he is the first person from Trenton, NJ to run for US Senate. He is the host of the *On Fire Show*. He has been featured in the *New York Times*, *The Daily Beast*, *NY Daily News*, *USA Today*, *Twiggs Café Radio.com*, *PoliticIt.com*, *IQ 106.9 FM*, *Philly Channel 6*, *WZBN News 12*, *Comcast Newsmakers*, *NJN*, *Trentonian*, *Trenton Times*, *Star Ledger*, *National Korean Newspaper*, *Ernest Hancock on LRN,FM*, *The Philly Tribune*, and *The Nubian News*. Brooks is in the Library of Congress. He is rated in the top 100 on "Top Talk Radio Conservative Radio Host".

ABOUT THE AUTHOR
STEPEN MARTINO

Stephen Martino is an Amazon bestselling author and physician who has written the fast-paced *Alex Pella* novel series, which include *The New Reality, The Hidden Reality,* and *The Final Reality. The New Reality* became an Amazon bestseller and a winner of the 2020 New York City Big Book Distinguished Favorite, while *The Final Reality* went on to win a Gold medal for Thrillers at the FAPA awards and was a winner of the CYGNUS Book Awards for Science Fiction.

A member of the International Thriller Writers, Martino's action-political thrillers are often compared to such substantive novels as the *Sigma Series* by James Rollins, novels by Isaac Asimov, the *Da Vinci Code* by Dan Brown, and *The Andromeda Strain* by fellow physician, Michael Crichton.

His books have been featured on numerous blogs across the United States and Europe including *Indigo Quill, Writer's Life, Confessions of a Reader, As the Page Turns, I Heart Reading,* and *Mary's Cup of Tea* among others.

Made in the USA
Columbia, SC
09 October 2024

43999301R00057